# Surviving Your Student Loans

I have used my best efforts in researching the information contained in this book. However, programs change and regulations are subject to interpretation. The author and the publisher specifically disclaim any responsibility or any liability for loss or risk – personal or otherwise – which may be incurred as a consequence, either direct or indirect, of the use or application of information contained in this book. The reader is advised to contact his or her lender for the most current information on eligibility for deferments, discharges, and forbearances. The examples in this book are fictitious. Any similarity to real persons, living or dead, is coincidental and not intended by the author.

-Nancy Mitchell

# Surviving Your Student Loans

*Nancy Mitchell*

*This book is dedicated to Don and Joan Mitchell, two of the most wonderful people in the world. It is further dedicated to the thousands of hard working financial aid professionals who spend their lives looking for ways to help people – young and old – continue their educations.*

# Acknowledgements

It is impossible to adequately thank everyone who had an influence on the writing of this book. First and foremost, my editor, friend, and sister-in-love, Dr. Joan L. Mitchell, an IBM Fellow. Joan not only encouraged me and supported me emotionally through her experience as an editor and author of technical books, she also provided a grant of money which allowed me to quit my day job and spend full time writing. There will never be enough 'thank yous' for that gift.

Second, but not really, is my husband Don Mitchell, who has always stood foursquare behind me in my desire to write. Besides his unfailing encouragement, Don pitched in to help with the research required in order to make this project complete.

My dear friend Ruth Proud Sheehy went through one of the earlier drafts with the proverbial fine-toothed comb. Ruth un-split my infinitives, and beat me about the head and ears to drop the use of vague pronouns and replace them with specific nouns. She even did a little re-writing whenever she found a passage unclear. Which, of course, led me to rewrite her rewrites, since I had apparently been unclear enough she did not understand what I meant. Thank you, Ruth, for always believing in me and making me strive harder than I ever wanted to.

SallieMae, for whom I worked for a period of time, brought to my attention the need for such a book. Having completed my degree on the 'pay as you go' plan, I was unaware of the vast number of people struggling to repay the loans they took out in order to obtain their educations. The daily pain of working as a default prevention specialist led me to write this book. It should be noted, neither Sallie Mae, nor any of the other guarantors or lenders with whom I was in contact have edited or reviewed this book, nor do they necessarily subscribe to the opinions stated here.

Thanks to the many people who reviewed the draft and sent me corrections. Their help and encouragement was invaluable.

Confidentiality and privacy laws prohibit me from naming any of the hundreds of harried borrowers floundering in student loan debt who begged me to put simple explanations in writing. I have tried to keep it simple, and this book was written for and because of those people. You know who you are and I sincerely hope it helps.

# Preface

This book was written for everyone – student or parent – who has or will have student loans. It is designed to help people avoid the agony of mismanaging their loans. If you know what you are getting into, you can better plan for the future. If you already have student loans, you need to know how to manage them to your best advantage.

I spent a period of time working as a default prevention specialist – a debt collector – for student loans. This book was born from the heartache of spending ten hours a day throwing lifelines to those who were drowning in their student loans.

The major problem I encountered in student loan default prevention was simply that many people do not know what options are available to them. It is not surprising in a world of fluctuating economies that most people seem to have difficulty keeping up with their financial obligations at one time or another. The problem may be unemployment, or under-employment, or over-spending, or simple unawareness that a payment has become due and payable. In my position as a collection agent, the supervisor often bewailed the fact I spent too much time on each call, explaining the ways in which people could ease their financial burdens. From the other end of the telephone, I received daily requests begging me to write a book, to put my knowledge into simple, easy to understand terms.

Since leaving that position, I have used my best efforts to research the subject thoroughly and provide the most accurate information available. However, programs change. This book can only provide the starting place for you, the borrower, in the management of your debts. I went back and forth over the idea of including the necessary forms in this book, and finally decided not to do so. The forms change too frequently, and if you were to use what I could include, the likelihood is your request would be denied. The most current forms can be readily obtained from your lender or at www.dlssonline.com/defer. This site also includes instructions for completing the forms.

Student loans are a wonderful way to pay for your education. They allow you to go to school now, and pay for it later. Presumably, later you will be better able to pay. Student loans also have a multitude of ways to put off that later payment, and it is the ease with which payments can be delayed which frequently causes problems for people. The purpose of this book is to educate you so you don't experience those problems.

The book is laid out simply, with an overview of student loans in general (including some of the common misconceptions people have) and a brief review of compound interest in the Introduction.

Chapter 1 covers the Master Promissory Note (MPN). This is the contract underlying all federally guaranteed student loans. I point out a few of the issues which most people tend to miss, ignore, or forget regarding their student loans. Since the Master Promissory Note changes with each change in loan programs, you must refer to your copy in order to know exactly what you signed.

Next, I describe the types of student loans available and some of the characteristics of each. The book concentrates on the most common types of federally guaranteed student loans, but brief mention is given to some of the other programs. The third chapter covers delinquency and default. I will point out the consequences of each and the timeline involved

Chapters 4 and 5 address the cures for delinquency – deferment and forbearance. Of course, payment is always the best cure, but if you had the money you wouldn't be delinquent.

The next chapter outlines the ways in which loans can be discharged. There are numerous ways to discharge both Stafford/Direct loans and Perkins loans, but in most cases, they are not the same ways.

Chapter 7 will go into the benefits of consolidation, and some of the limitations you may experience.

Chapter 8 tells you about the payment options available to you. Most lenders offer more than just the standard ten-year repayment plan.

Once you have the basics of student loans, Chapter 9 illustrates the use of those basics through examples. Many of you may find it helpful to skip straight to Chapter 9 and read the examples first, and then go back to the pertinent chapters to pick up the details about deferments, forbearances, loan types, and so on.

Finally, Chapter 10 details loan management ideas to help you avoid the need to use either deferment or forbearance.

Following the text of the book, I have added a couple of appendices. Acronyms, the wonderful shorthand common to every field of endeavor and understood by no one outside the field, are included as Appendix A. Appendix B is a glossary of commonly used terms. You can thank my many reviewers for the glossary. I received repeated requests to create a glossary for the convenience of those who have not spent hours, days, and months living with these concepts.

This book was conceived as a way to help people who are already in trouble with their loans to get out of trouble. I tried to address the issues I came across most frequently in my position as a default prevention specialist. The book's secondary purpose – equally important – is to help those who are not in trouble with their loans to stay out of trouble. I don't have any 'insiders' tricks' to help you avoid paying your loans back. *There aren't any 'insiders' tricks'.* What I can give you is information, so you can make rational, informed decisions.

I have used my best efforts in researching the information contained in this book. However, programs change and regulations are subject to interpretation. The author and the publisher specifically disclaim any responsibility for or any liability for loss or risk – personal or otherwise – which may be incurred as a consequence, either direct or indirect, of the use or application of information contained in this book. The reader is advised to contact his or her lender for the most current information on eligibility for deferments, discharges, and forbearances.

# Table of Contents

# Introduction

An article in **The Wall Street Journal**[i] cites student lender Nellie Mae as saying the average student-loan debt is nearly $ 28,000. If you are one of the millions who need help getting out of financial difficulty because you have lost or misplaced the information you need about your student loans, then this book is a simple guide out of your dilemma. (*Hopefully* you are reading this book long before your loans ever become a problem for you.)

## Basic Loan Types

Since student loans have their own vocabulary, I will give you a very basic overview here of the loan types available. More detailed descriptions will follow in the chapter on loan types.

Stafford loans are available to students without any credit qualification. Stafford loans may be subsidized or unsubsidized, based on need.

Direct loans (also called William G. Ford loans) are very similar to Stafford loans, but the loan comes directly from the government rather than from a student loan lender.

PLUS (Parental Loans for Undergraduate Students) are loans taken out by parents on behalf of students in order to fulfill their Expected Family Contribution.

Federal Supplemental Loans for Students (SLS loans) are no longer available, but were once used to fill the gap between grants and scholarships and available funds from family. They have been replaced by unsubsidized Stafford loans.

Perkins loans are made by the school. As you will notice in later chapters, all Perkins deferment and discharge forms must be obtained from the lending school.

Alternative loans are private loans made by banks and lending institutions. Many of these lenders allow delay of payment in some way, but any forms required must be obtained from your lender.

## Myths and Misconceptions

*Myth:* I don't have to make any payments until after I graduate.

*Reality:* While you are enrolled in classes *at least half time* your loans *may* qualify for in-school deferment. If your loans are subsidized, the government will pay your interest during deferment. If your loans are not subsidized, you are responsible for the interest at all times. If you do not pay the interest while in deferment, the interest will capitalize. *If you fail to qualify for the in-school deferment, your loans go into repayment.* For specific information about your grace period, refer to your Master Promissory Note.

*Myth:* I have six (or nine) months after graduation before I have to make payments.

*Reality:* You have *up to* six or nine months after *dropping below half-time enrollment* before you must begin repaying your loans. This is a one-time deal, no saving up the unused time for later. If you drop out for a semester, you use your grace period in three months – not six or nine. Once again, refer to your Master Promissory Note.

*Myth:* I don't have to make payments on the PLUS loans I took out for my son until after he graduates.

*Reality:* If the initial disbursement and MPN (Master Promissory Note) predate 1986, you may defer your payments. However, all PLUS loans are unsubsidized loans so interest will accrue and capitalize. If the initial disbursement and MPN *do not* predate 1986, the *borrower* must be enrolled at least half-time in order to qualify to defer the loan. Refer to Chapter 4, Deferments. You may be thinking of forbearance rather than deferment. (*Deferment is permission to take time off from making payments if you meet certain qualifications set by the government. Forbearance is the lender's permission to take time off from making payments, if you meet their qualifications. During deferment, the government may be making your interest payments. During forbearance, the interest accrues, is added to the loan balance, and thereafter you pay interest on the interest – capitalization.*)

*Myth:* Once I graduate I plan to transfer all those PLUS loans my parents took out into my name.

*Reality:* Your parents applied for and agreed to pay those loans. Your lender is not likely to agree to a substitution of borrower. The only reasonable way to transfer the indebtedness from your parents to you is to arrange for a personal loan and use the funds to pay off the PLUS loans. Since the PLUS loans probably carry a lower interest rate than you can get on a personal loan, this does not make economic sense. Make the payments for your parents, but don't depend on the idea of transferring the loan.

*Myth:* After I graduate, I plan to consolidate my parent's PLUS loans with my Stafford loans so I'll only have one payment.

*Reality:* You still won't be able to transfer those PLUS loans into your name. Consolidation is probably a good idea, both for you and for your parents, but there will still be two loans – one for you and one for your parents. Refer to Chapter 7, Consolidation.

*Myth:* Nobody pays their student loans back. I'll just file bankruptcy.

*Reality*: Because this was common practice back in the sixties and seventies, the government tightened up on that loophole. In most cases student loans are excluded from bankruptcy. In order to have them discharged in this manner, you will need to prove *undue* hardship. Refer to Chapter 6, Loan Discharges.

*Myth:* I don't qualify for an unemployment deferment because I've never been employed.

*Reality:* You might qualify for the deferment. Are you actively looking for work? Are you registered with an employment agency? This is not about qualifying for state unemployment benefits (although if you are receiving unemployment benefits, you probably qualify for the deferment). Refer to Chapter 4, Deferments.

*Myth:* I don't have to worry about it anymore because the court awarded my student loan debt to my spouse in our divorce.

*Reality:* Your lender was not a party to the proceeding. Your lender isn't going to take action against your spouse in the event of a delinquency or default.

Your spouse owes the debt (money) to *you*, and you owe it to *your lender*. If your spouse does not make the required payments, it is *your* credit which will be affected. Consult with your attorney and see about arranging to have the payments sent to you so you can be sure they are sent to the lender.

# Interest

*The price you pay to borrow money*

We all understand when you borrow money you are expected to pay interest on the loan, unless, of course, you borrow the money from generous parents or grandparents.

Interest on a loan may be in the form of *simple* interest. In the case of simple interest, a $10,000 loan bearing a note rate of 10% will earn $1,000 in interest for the lender; therefore at the end of one year you will be required to pay back $11,000. If the term of the note is two years, you would be required to pay back $12,000, and so on.

Simple interest is a fairly simple concept to understand. Unfortunately, most notes do not bear simple interest. If you look at the disclosure statements you receive when you apply for a home loan, you will find with a fully amortized thirty year mortgage of $100,000 bearing a note rate of 10% per annum, you will eventually pay back somewhere in the neighborhood of $300,000. This is a simplification of the numbers involved, and not intended to be accurate, but you get the idea.

## The Magic of Compounding

From times before the pioneers and up through the era of the Baby-Boomers, children learned about the magic of compounding from their parents or in elementary school. Unfortunately for later generations, there has been less emphasis placed on saving and debt-management. Many young people today do not have a thorough grasp of those concepts. As for myself, I first learned about interest when I was in third grade. My teacher explained to me if I put $1 in a bank account on January first, and my account carried an interest rate of 10%, then on January 1$^{st}$ of the following year, I would have a whole $1.10! And, she further explained, if I left the money in the bank, and never added to it, on the following January 1$^{st}$, I would have $1.21 in the bank (and so on into perpetuity). Of course, the teacher's explanation only compounded the interest annually, but then, she was explaining the idea to an eight-year old. Nowadays, your financial planner will put the concept in simpler terms by explaining the Rule of 72.

Under the Rule of 72, funds invested at 10% will double in 7.2 years if left alone. And the new balance will double again in another 7.2 years if left invested at the same rate of return. Then the financial planner will go further and explain if you add to your investment each year, the balance grows even faster. If you fund your 401k or your IRA in your early years, the compounding will make you rich in your retirement years.

Figure 1 below shows the value of a $10,000 investment compounding quarterly over a period of seven years. The top line shows a return rate of 10%, the center line shows 8%, and the bottom line shows 4%. Obviously if you have invested your funds, you would prefer they earn 10%, since the value of your investment very nearly doubles in the seven years I show. On the other hand, if you are a borrower and the graph shows the principal balance of your loans while you aren't making payments, you'd better *hope* the interest rate is only 4%.

**Figure 1: Compounding at 4%, 8%, and 10% Interest**

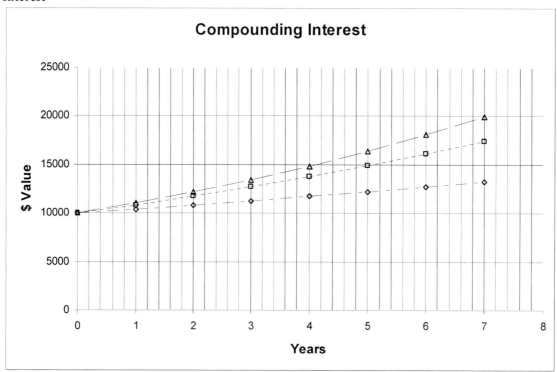

**The Same Thing Happens in Reverse**

The point of this explanation is the same thing can happen to you in *reverse*. If you make no payments on a loan at 10%, your balance will double in 7.2 years. If you make interest-only payments on the same loan you will never actually get the loan paid off, but the balance will not grow.

---

**Remember, the Rule of 72 Works in Reverse**

**If you make no payments on an unpaid loan at 10% per annum, your loan balance will *double* in 7.2 years and *double again* in another 7.2 years.**

---

Now let's look at some numbers. The maximum amount of subsidized and unsubsidized loans available to a *dependent* student through the Stafford loan programs is $23,000 during their undergraduate studies. As previously mentioned, there are additional sources of funding available to fill the gap between the Stafford loan and the actual cost of education. For demonstration purposes I will use a loan amount of $10,000.

The interest rate on Stafford (and Direct) loans is determined by the government. Stafford (and Direct) loans disbursed after 10/1/98 carry a variable rate. The annual rate is determined in July for the following year. Over the past twenty-five years, rates have been high (double-digits) and they have been low (single-digit). As of this writing, student loan interest rates are at historical lows (2.82% during school, 3.42% in repayment for loans disbursed after July 1, 1998), however, student loan rates are subject to change. The rate is based on the 91-Day T-Bill plus 1.7% while the student is in school, grace period, or deferment and 91-Day T-Bill plus 2.3% during repayment. The interest rate on these loans is capped at 8.25%.[ii] The interest rate on Perkins loans is fixed at 5%.[iii]

Because most borrowers have both subsidized and unsubsidized loans, I will be using an 8% rate for deferments and a 10% rate for forbearances even though these are not the current rates. This will both simplify the calculations and provide dramatic impact. Hopefully the interest rate applied to *your* loans will never approach these numbers, but in my former life as a bill collector (default prevention), I frequently dealt with borrowers who were and are paying these high rates on older loans.

## Table 1: Interest Capitalized on $10,000 for 1 Year

|  | $1^{st}$ qtr | $2^{nd}$ qtr | $3^{rd}$ qtr | $4^{th}$ qtr | Total interest |
|---|---|---|---|---|---|
| **Deferment @ 8%** | $200.00 | $204.00 | $208.08 | $212.24 | $824.32 |
| **Forbearance @10%** | 250.00 | 256.25 | 262.66 | 269.33 | 1,038.24 |

Table 1 shows the interest which will be capitalized, quarterly and for the full year if you do not make payments during the year. The numbers also demonstrate the effect of *compounding* the interest – in other words, when you pay interest on interest.

With simple interest and an 8% note rate, a $10,000 loan would grow to $10,800 in one year. But compounding the interest means paying interest on the interest. Because the interest on the loan is capitalized quarterly, and thereafter the lender charges interest on the capitalized interest, the loan balance grows to $10,824.32.

The second point to be made in this demonstration is the difference between *deferment* and *forbearance*. As previously noted, most people have a combination of both subsidized and unsubsidized loans. During forbearance, interest on all loans accrues, and is capitalized and compounded; but during deferment, the government pays the interest on the subsidized portions of your loans. In Table 1 above, the beginning interest amounted to $200 and $250 respectively, and the accrued interest ($200 or $250) continued to accrue interest as time went on.

Table 2 gives you the same information as was in Figure 1 shown earlier – but with the addition of the monthly payments due. Since the standard repayment plan for student loans will fully amortize the loan in 10 years, the payment goes up with each year the loan remains in forbearance

Table 2: $10,000 balance, no payments for 7 years, @ 4%, 8%, and 10%

| Year | 4% | | 8% | | 10% | |
|---|---|---|---|---|---|---|
| | **balance** | **pmt** | **balance** | **pmt** | **balance** | **pmt** |
| 0 | $10,000.00 | $101.25 | $10,000.00 | $121.33 | $10,000.00 | $132.15 |
| 1 | 10,406.04 | 105.36 | 10,824.32 | 131.33 | 11,038.13 | 145.87 |
| 2 | 10,828.57 | 109.63 | 11,716.59 | 142.15 | 12,184.03 | 161.61 |
| 3 | 11,268.25 | 114.09 | 12,682.42 | 153.87 | 13,448.89 | 177.73 |
| 4 | 11,725.79 | 118.72 | 13,727.86 | 166.56 | 14,845.06 | 196.18 |
| 5 | 12,201.90 | 123.54 | 14,859.47 | 180.29 | 16,386.16 | 216.54 |
| 6 | 12,697.35 | 128.55 | 16,084.37 | 195.15 | 18,087.25 | 239.02 |
| 7 | 13,212,91 | 133.77 | 17,410.24 | 211.23 | 19,964.94 | 263.84 |

[i] Kelly K. Spors, "Nursing a Debt Hangover From College", *The Wall Street Journal* WSJ pg 3, April 25, 2004.
[ii] http://studentloan.citibank.com
[iii] http://studentaid.ed.gov.students

# Chapter 1:  Master Promissory Note

When you applied for your student loans, you were given a stack of supporting documentation about twelve inches high.  The stack may have included copies of copies of copies of originals, and been virtually unreadable.  Most likely you did not have the time (or the desire) to read it anyway.  You were registering for classes, and beginning classes, and you had so much important material to read you probably placed the loan information on the back burner to read at a later time.  If you are like most people, that later time never arrived.  Bear with me while I review the most important things that many people paid no attention to when they took out their student loans.

## Master Promissory Note Covers all Loans

All of your federally guaranteed student loans with a single lender are covered under a single Master Promissory Note[iv] (MPN).  A *Master Promissory Note* is a promise to pay back your loans – a one-time IOU.  You signed the Master Promissory Note only once and it applied to all the disbursements.  *Disbursements* are loan moneys you received (or which were paid on your behalf) during the term of your enrollments in school.  The only time this Master Promissory Note ceases to be applicable is when you completely pay off your student loans.  In that case, if you later decide to return to school and seek new loans, you will need to execute a new MPN.

If you sign a Master Promissory Note with one lender, and later decide to obtain federal student loans from a different lender, you must execute a new MPN.  However, unless you have paid off all loans received under the first MPN, *the terms and conditions of the first MPN continue to apply* – even if the terms and conditions on the new MPN you signed are different.

This is a very important point.  ***The date of your MPN and your initial loan disbursement governs the rules for your deferments.***  If your first disbursement was prior to January 1993, you qualify for one set of deferments, and if after January 1993, another set applies.

## Repayment

When you took out your student loans, the financial aid office may have told you nothing had to be repaid until you finished school. This statement is quite correct as far as it goes. What may not have been emphasized strongly enough is if you take a semester off from classes, or if you drop below half time enrollment, your loan is treated *as if you have finished school*. Finishing school does not necessarily mean graduating from school. Some financial aid officers explain in detail how taking time off from school will effect repayment of your loan, while others expect you to read and understand the supporting documentation you received.

## The Lender has the Right to Sell or Assign your Loans

Your MPN grants to your lender the right to sell or assign your loan(s) to another lender at their discretion. Your lender may choose to sell some of your loans (disbursements), but perhaps not all of them. They may sell your loans to more than one lender. If and when your loans are transferred, your lender is required to notify you of the change. Notification is made by first class mail to the last address you gave them. If you moved without notifying your lender, their notices of loan transfer may not find you until you are already delinquent in your payments.

## Interest Accrues from Date of Disbursement

Your MPN provides for interest to accrue (accumulate) from the date of initial loan disbursement. This means while you are in school, the interest is adding up on your loan.

If your loans are *subsidized*, the government will be paying the interest on your loans while you are in school at least half-time.

If your loans are *unsubsidized*, the government will not pay your interest at any time. You have agreed to begin making payments on your unsubsidized loan from the date of disbursement unless you also arrange for an "in-school deferment". *Deferment* is a postponement of loan payments until a later time. See the Chapter on deferments for more information.

For many students, the financial aid package includes a mix of the following:
- Grants – grants are gifts which do not have to be repaid;
- Subsidized loans – the interest on subsidized loans is paid by the government while you are in deferment; and
- Unsubsidized loans – the interest on unsubsidized loans accrues and is capitalized during all periods of nonpayment.

If you have any doubts about the kinds of loans you received, check with your lender. The lender's records will show which of your loans are subsidized and which are not. You can also go to www.nslds.ed.gov. This is the national student loan data system. This system will have information on all of your current student loans.

## Repayment Begins Immediately upon Disbursement

Your MPN provides for repayment to begin immediately upon loan disbursement. Then your school certifies your enrollment status, and your school arranges for your student loans to be placed in deferment while you attend school at least half time. However, if you take a semester off, or change schools, or drop below half time enrollment for any reason, you enter into your "grace period". Your *grace period* is the interval of time between the leaving of school and the beginning of your loan repayment. Any loans you had when you took time out from classes will be in repayment six or nine months after you first stopped out. If you return to school, your loans can be placed back into deferment, but when your deferment is up, you do not get another grace period on those loans. It is not uncommon for individuals to have some loans in repayment and others in 'grace'.

## Payments are Applied to Fees, Interest, and then Principal

Your MPN outlines the manner in which payments on your student loans are to be applied, including interest, late fees and collection costs. The lender decides the order in which the payments are *actually* applied.

Exclusive of refunds, payments made on your student loans can be applied *first* to late fees and collection costs, then to accrued interest, and last to principal. If you get behind, contact your lender immediately. They can help you get current. They have even been known to waive late fees and collection costs when a borrower makes the effort to keep in contact with them and keep them apprised of exigent circumstances.

## Your Loan Can be Accelerated

Your MPN provides for acceleration of the loan. *Acceleration of the loan means the loan immediately becomes all due and payable.* If you take out a student loan, and then do not enroll at least half time at the school which certified your eligibility, the loan becomes immediately all due and payable.

### Educational Purposes Only

If you fail to use the loan proceeds solely for educational purposes, the loan may be accelerated and become all due and payable. 'Educational purposes' is a fairly broad description and includes tuition, room and board, institutional fees, books, supplies, equipment, dependent child care, transportation, commuting expenses, rental or purchase of a personal computer, origination and guarantee fees and other documented and authorized costs. It is not likely to include a trip to Tahiti for Spring Break, although it might cover a trip to Bora Bora for research relating to your doctoral thesis. If you have any questions about the use to which you plan to put your loan proceeds, check with your lender.

### False Representations

If you make false representations in order to obtain the loan, the loan becomes all due and payable (presumably as soon as the lender finds out about the fraud). Since the information on your Free Application for Federal Student Aid (FAFSA) is the basis for determining your eligibility for student loans and grants, and since all the information contained in the FAFSA will be verified by the financial aid office, you need to be certain it is correct. Depending upon the severity of the fraud involved, you could be subject to criminal charges, but this would not be a normal result. In most cases, the financial aid office will simply help you to correct the misinformation – after all, everybody makes mistakes – and your loan eligibility will be adjusted accordingly.

## Default

Finally, if you default, the loan becomes all due and payable. There is a difference between defaulting on the loan and being delinquent (late) on the loan. According to your MPN, if you fail to make your payments when due for 270 days (for monthly installment payments), or 330 days (if your payment schedule is less frequent than monthly) the loan may be considered to be in default.

If default should occur, the loan is all due and payable, and you will have incurred substantial late fees and collection fees. If fact, collection fees may be as much as 25% of the *original* principal amount. So when you get into the home stretch, and you only owe $1,000 on what started out as $46,000 in loans, don't choke at the finish. You could end up owing an additional $11,500 in collection fees!

### Keep in Touch With Your Lender

Your MPN requires you to keep your lender apprised of your current address and status. Notifying your lender of any change of address becomes particularly critical when you graduate from school and relocate. You are responsible for the payments (and late fees) even if you never receive the notices your lender sends.

If you are unable to locate a copy of the MPN you actually signed, contact your lender. Your lender has an original of the document you signed and will be able to provide you with a copy.

# Be Aware of Changes

As previously mentioned, the date of your MPN and your first disbursement governs the set of rules and regulations which apply to your loans. The Higher Education Act of 1965, Part B of Title IV authorizes the Federal Family Education Loan Program (FFELP) and is the basis for all federally guaranteed student loans. However, the Department of Education and Congress have been fine-tuning the program ever since.

Major changes occurred in 1986, when they determined PLUS loans should not be eligible for deferment simply because the student for whom the loans were taken out was in school. After all, the parent is the responsible party on a PLUS loan, and presumably the parent is working and earning an income, so why defer the loan?

At some point Congress and the Department of Education came up with a long list of reasons to defer payment on the loans. Most of those were public service career related deferments, but they also included a couple of new baby deferments.

In 1993 they decided they could simplify matters by doing away with the various career-related and new baby deferments and simply bundle them all under economic hardship. The economic hardship deferment is much broader in scope and covers the needs of more people. However, if your first loan was disbursed prior to 1993 you don't qualify for the economic hardship deferment because it did not exist at the time you entered into your contract. So they added an economic hardship forbearance.

In 1994 they eliminated SLS loans and Student Plus loans and raised the limits on unsubsidized Stafford loans.

In 1998 they instituted a program for partial forgiveness of Stafford loans for teachers who meet certain requirements. Teachers whose Stafford loans pre-date 1998 are currently out of luck.

In 1998 they made the loan forgiveness programs and some deferments for Perkins loans retroactive as they relate to the *initial disbursements*, but not retroactive as they relate to *years of service*.

In 2002 the Permanent Disability Discharge became *conditional* for three years with re-certification required.

2004. An article in the Las Vegas Review Journal[v] indicates Congress *will be* eliminating the fixed-rate consolidation option for student loans. Although loans will still be eligible for consolidation, the interest rate after consolidation will remain variable and, presumably, tied to the Treasury Bill rate. There is speculation over the interest rate cap which will be applied. One group is working for a 6.8% cap, while another wishes to maintain the current cap of 8.25%. The consensus seems to be the fixed-rate option will become a thing of the past for loans issued after July 2006.

July 2005. Congress moved more quickly than expected. Loans consolidated after June 30, 2005 will carry a variable interest rate.

Congress is working on reauthorization even as I write, so who knows what other changes may take place next month or next year? The 1965 Act was a good starting place and is continually in the process of refinement. For updated information and current forms go to www.studentaid.ed.gov. This website has links which will take you to the most recent news.

---

[iv] All information pertaining to the MPN is taken from the most recent version (2000) of the MPN.

[v] Justin Pope, "Proposal Would End Fixed-Rate Consolidation", *Las Vegas Review-Journal*, p. 9A, June 7, 2004

# Chapter 2:  Types of Loans

There are several different types of student loans.  The most prevalent types are outlined here.

## Stafford Loans

The most common type of loan is the Stafford loan.  Stafford loans may be subsidized, in which case the government pays the interest while the borrower is in deferment, or they may be unsubsidized.  The government does not pay the interest on unsubsidized loans.

The amount of subsidized versus unsubsidized loans you receive is a factor of need and is determined after you have completed your Free Application for Federal Student Aid (FAFSA).

During deferment (either in-school or other authorized delay of payment), the interest on unsubsidized loans accrues and is capitalized and added to the principal balance of the loan.  This means the loan balance will go up during periods of non-payment.  Thereafter, the lender will charge interest on the capitalized interest as well as on the initial principal.  (Compounding of interest was described in the Introduction.)

Interest rates on Stafford loans are variable, based on the 91-Day T-Bill rate plus a premium.  The rate for the year is set in July of each year.  More specific information is included later in this book.

Currently, a dependent student may borrow up to $23,000 in subsidized and unsubsidized Stafford loans during their undergraduate studies.  An independent student may borrow the same $23,000 in subsidized and unsubsidized loans, and an additional $23,000 in *unsubsidized* Stafford loans.

An independent student is at least 24 years old, married, a graduate or professional student, a veteran, an orphan, a ward of the court, or someone who has legal dependents other than a spouse at the time they apply for their Stafford loans.[vi]

Graduate and professional students may continue their education with federally guaranteed loans of up to $18,500 per year (maximum $8,500 subsidized and $10,000 unsubsidized). The cumulative total of their graduate/professional school loans (with the exception of some health care professions) can be no more than $138,500. These loans are subject to deferment and forbearance.

## Direct Loans

Direct loans, also known as William D. Ford loans, have the same deferment rules, interest rate, and loan limits as Stafford loans. The biggest difference between a Direct loan and a Stafford loan is the source of the funds involved. Stafford loans are made by authorized student loan lenders and guaranteed by the federal government. Direct loans are actually made by the government. Both programs carry the same lifetime loan amounts, and the limits aggregate. An independent student cannot borrow $ 46,000 (subsidized and unsubsidized) in Stafford loans and another $46,000 in Direct loans. He or she can, however, borrow $40,000 in Stafford loans and another $6,000 in Direct loans, or any other combination which adds up to no more than $46,000. There are two other major differences between Stafford and Direct loans. When the government established the Direct loan program, they decided to give themselves a competitive advantage over the private lenders. This is because the primary reason for establishing the program was to allow the government to participate in the profits to be made from student loans. However, all other things being equal, most of us prefer to deal with private enterprise rather than federal bureaucrats. The only way the government could ensure they would get any student loan business was to give themselves programs not available to private lenders. The two major differences are 1) the income-contingent repayment plan, and 2) certain consolidation advantages[vii]. The income-contingent payment option is covered in Chapter 8, and the differences in consolidation are covered in Chapter 7. Because of these differences, it is very important for borrowers to be aware of the *single lender rule* (for Stafford loans). Try to have at least two different lenders on your student loans. Since lenders tend to sell their loans to one another, you probably want to have at least one Direct loan (which is unlikely to be sold).

# PLUS Loans

The next major grouping of federal student loans is the Parental Loans for Undergraduate Students (PLUS) loan group. PLUS loans are designed to help families meet their Expected Family Contribution (EFC), as defined by the government.

The government has determined parents are responsible for helping their children to become educated, productive individuals, and they have created a formula to determine how much a family should contribute based upon family income, size, and the number of young people a family has in college at any given time. EFC is determined from the FAFSA.

PLUS loans are *never* subsidized loans, and they carry a slightly higher rate of interest than Stafford and Direct loans. Generally speaking however, the rate of interest is lower than would be available to most borrowers on a simple signature loan. PLUS loans may be eligible for deferment and forbearance. However since they are not subsidized, the government does not pay the interest during deferment. The deferment qualifications must be met by the borrower (parent), not the student. Only PLUS loans disbursed prior to 1986 qualify for an in-school deferment when the borrower (parent) is not the one in school.

PLUS loans require a credit check and acceptable credit history. They are available from either private student loan lenders or from the government through their Direct loan program. They are federally guaranteed, which accounts for the lower than market interest rate and the minimal credit qualification. As mentioned later, the student cannot consolidate the parent loans after graduation. The borrowing parent remains responsible for the loan until it has been paid off, even if the student has actually taken on the burden of making the payments.

# SLS Loans and Student PLUS Loans

Federal Supplemental Loans for Students (SLS) and Student PLUS Loans were discontinued in 1994 and replaced by unsubsidized Stafford loans. SLS loans and Student PLUS Loans were only available to credit-worthy students. For those of you who have not yet completely paid off your SLS loans or Student PLUS loans, deferment and forbearance information is available from your lender.  These were not subsidized loans so interest accrues and is capitalized during either deferment or forbearance.

## HEAL and Federal Nursing Loans

Federal Nursing Loans and Health Education Assistance Loans (HEAL) are specific to the health care industries; doctors and nurses, chiropractors and dentists and any of the associated fields.  These loans may qualify for deferment and forbearance.  You must contact your lender for specific information regarding these types of loans.  HEAL loans are not available at this time[viii], but many of the older loans have not yet been repaid.

## Perkins Loans

Perkins Loans are low interest loans made by the school to undergraduate and graduate students with financial needs.  The interest rate on Perkins loans is currently quoted on the Department of Education website[ix] at 5%.  The loan funds are borrowed from the government, with the school contributing a share, rather than borrowed from a student loan lender.  The funds available to lend each year are severely limited.

Undergraduate students may borrow up to $4,000 per year, with a lifetime maximum of $20,000.  Graduate students may borrow up to $6,000 per year, with an aggregate total (graduate and undergraduate borrowing) of $40,000. Perkins loans qualify for deferment, forbearance (three years maximum), and total or partial discharge in certain circumstances.  Perkins loans also carry a nine month grace period (as opposed to a six month grace period on the Stafford loans).  There is a ten year re-payment period on Perkins loans.  Deferment and forbearance are handled through the school from which you obtain the loan, or through the servicing agency to which your school has assigned the loan.

Since Perkins loans may be discharged or partially discharged in exchange for years spent in certain public service occupations, they may be much more desirable than Stafford or Direct (Ford) loans.  However, they are not available from all schools, and the annual budget for each participating school is limited.

If you are planning a career in education, law enforcement, nursing, or other public service fields, you should explore your Perkins loan options carefully.

## Alternative Loans

Another category is the private loan group. Private loans are readily available from most private student-loan lenders. Each bank sets its own lending guidelines, including the amounts they are willing to lend and the level of credit screening they require.

Private loans are not subsidized, and private loans are not guaranteed by the federal government. Each lender determines whether deferments and or forbearance will be available and under what terms.

Many lenders allow for deferral of payments while the student is in school, and many allow for later periods of 'time off' due to exigent circumstances. However, during these periods of deferment or forbearance, the interest will continue to accrue and capitalize in accordance with the lender's policies.

Private loans are not subsidized, so taking time off from making payments is a dangerous option. It is important to note, *private loans may not be consolidated with federal loans.*

## State Programs

Most states have some type of financial aid available to students, either in the form of loans or grants. There is an excellent source available for information on those programs. Carlyn Foshee Chatfield, formerly the Assistant Director of Student Financial Services at Rice University wrote a book entitled *Financial Aid 101*. Her Appendix D is a listing by state of such special programs. For example, Alabama has a G.I. Dependents Scholarship Program awarding up to $7,000.[x] Ms. Chatfield's book is primarily concerned with the processes of financial aid, and the types of aid available. It identifies the kinds of aid a student may hope for – grants (both institutional and federal), scholarships, and loans – and explains the FAFSA.

Table 3 lists the current loan limits for Stafford, Direct, and Perkins loans.

## Table 3: Maximum loan limits

| Type of loan | Subsidized[*] | Lifetime[**] Maximum Undergraduate | Lifetime Maximum Graduate | Deferments Available |
|---|---|---|---|---|
| Stafford | Maybe | $ 46,000 | $138,500 | Yes |
| Direct (Ford) | Maybe | $ 46,000 | $138,500 | Yes |
| Perkins | Maybe | $ 20,000 | $ 20,000 | Yes |
| PLUS | No | --- | --- | Yes[***] |
| HEAL | Maybe | --- | --- | Yes |
| SLS/Student PLUS | No | --- | --- | Yes[***] |
| Private | No | Varies | Varies | Maybe[****] |

[vi] Current information is available on-line at http://studentaid.ed.gov/students.

[vii] http://www.dlssonline.com

[viii] Gen and Kelly Tanabe, *1001 Ways to Pay for College*, SuperCollege, LLC, p. 264 (2003).

[ix] http://studentaid.ed.gov/students/publications.

[x] Carlyn Foshee Chatfield, *Financial Aid 101*, Thomson-Peterson p.202 (2004).

[*] the government pays the interest during deferment.

[**] Assumes an independent student. Aggregate total of both subsidized and unsubsidized loans.

[***] The government does not pay the interest on unsubsidized loans.

[****] The government does not pay the interest on private loans. Lender may allow deferral of payments.

# Chapter 3: Default and Delinquency

*When you don't make your payments on time*

## A Lender's Timeline

The first thing you need to realize is your lender may count time differently from you and me. Your payment is due on its due date, not within a few days after its due date. Your repayment period begins the first day after your grace period expires, not thirty days after your grace period expires[xi]. PLUS loan payments are due 60 days after disbursement unless you have arranged for deferment or forbearance.

If you miss a payment due date, the lender *may* consider you thirty days late, even though you believe you are only one day late. If you miss a second payment, you may be sixty days late. If you miss a third payment, you may be ninety days late and the lender will likely report the delinquency to the credit bureaus.

Each lender sets its own policy for credit bureau reporting. Some report as early as sixty days, and most report by ninety days. A very few will wait until the following Monday after the ninetieth day to report the delinquent payments (for convenience of reporting).

*All* lenders report late payments to the credit bureaus. In fact, SallieMae, one of the nation's largest student loan lenders, recently lost a law suit because they were *not* reporting to all major credit bureaus.[xii] College graduates fresh out of school frequently have little or no credit other than their student loans. If the timely payment of their student loans is not accurately reported to all major credit bureaus, young adults may be unable to qualify for a home loan, due to the lack of this favorable credit history. Failure to report favorable credit accurately to all major credit bureaus was the basis of the law suit, and SallieMae is now ordered to report to all major credit bureaus. Since SallieMae (and other student-loan lenders) may not discriminate for or against borrowers in their reporting practices, they naturally report *adverse* credit to all major bureaus as well.

Adverse credit may not prevent you from being able to obtain a home loan or a vehicle loan, but it will affect your credit score, and therefore the interest rate you receive when you apply for major credit.

Once you have missed your second payment, your lender is required by Department of Education regulation to notify the guarantor on the loan that you are delinquent and in danger of defaulting on the loan.[xiii] Delinquency triggers those annoying phone calls, and the collection specialists continue to call and write until the loan is brought current, either through payment, deferment, or forbearance. *Forbearance is the lender's permission to delay your payments or make smaller payments.*

You should understand your lender has *no choice* but to report delinquencies and the guarantor's office has *no choice* but to begin collection efforts.

A default can occur after you have missed payments for a period of 270 days (nine months) on a loan on which payments are scheduled to occur monthly. If payments are scheduled less frequently, the default can occur after you have missed your payments for 330 days.

Your student loans are federally insured. If you default on the loan, and the guarantor is unsuccessful in their attempts to rehabilitate the loan, the guarantor must pay the lender for the loss they incur on the loan. The guarantor then seeks relief from the federal government for the loss incurred. The federal government then seeks relief from you, the borrower, for the loss incurred. Even before the lender reports you to the guarantor, they will begin their own collection efforts, through telephone calls and letters. The procedures are set by law, and neither the lender nor the guarantor is allowed to deviate from them.

## Table 4: Delinquency and Default

| Event | Consequence |
|---|---|
| Payment due | |
| Payment late (30+days) | Lender considers payment 30 days late |
| | Lender sends notice of delinquency to last known address |
| | Lender telephones last known number |
| Payment late (60 days) | Lender sends request for assistance to guarantor |
| | Lender continues to telephone last known number |
| Payment late (61+ days) | Guarantor begins calling last known number |
| | Guarantor sends notice of delinquency to all known addresses |
| | Guarantor calls references for address/telephone update |
| | Guarantor performs 'skip trace' to locate borrower |
| | Lender continues to telephone last known number |
| Payment late (270+ days) | Lender files notice of default |
| | Lender ceases collection efforts |
| | Guarantor continues to telephone all possible numbers |
| | Guarantor continues to send delinquency notices to all known addresses |
| | Guarantor reviews loan file for procedural accuracy |
| | Guarantor pays lender for defaulted loan |
| | Guarantor may attach wages |
| | Guarantor's collection efforts increase |
| | Guarantor may lien real estate holdings |

# Default has Consequences

## Seizure of State and Federal Income Tax Refunds

The consequences of a default on a student loan are very serious. If you were expecting a state or federal income tax refund, you will likely receive instead a letter stating your refund has been withheld to apply towards payment of your student loans.[xiv] Other federal or state payments may also be withheld in similar fashion. The guarantor, your lender, or the government may instigate legal action against you.

## Collection Fees

The guarantor has the right to add up to 25%[xiv] of the *original loan balance* in collection costs. You may also be required to pay attorney's fees for the guarantor or the lender or the government in their efforts to collect from you. This is in addition to accrued interest and late charges imposed by the lender. For example, if your original loan balance was $ 2,500 (per loan) and you have eight loans, then you have an original balance(s) of $20,000. You did not consolidate, but you did make regular payments and your remaining balance is less than $2,500. If your loan(s) defaults, some guarantors can collect up to $5,000 in loan fees, in addition to the remaining balance. Obviously you don't want this to happen.

## Wage Garnishment

If you default, your wages may be garnished, without judicial action[xv]. You have already given your lender the right to garnish your wages in this fashion, so there is no need for the lender or the guarantor or the government to go to court to enforce the garnishment. You may, however, appeal the garnishment. The forms necessary to do so are available on the internet at the Department of Education website[xvi]. Go to the Department of Education website and download the latest information. You will also need the Financial Disclosure form, which must be completed and submitted along with your request for a hearing.

## Higher Interest Rate

If you default on your student loans, you may be given the opportunity to rehabilitate the loans. However, the interest rate on your note may be raised, resulting in you paying more over the long run for the same funds.

## No More Financial Aid

If you default on your student loans, you may be denied additional financial aid if or when you attempt to return to school.[xv] Your diploma or credential may be withheld upon graduation. You may lose your professional license. Are you a doctor? A lawyer? A cosmetologist? Most states require you to have a professional license to practice in these and many other fields of endeavor.

Your loans may become ineligible for deferment or forbearance.

## Adverse Credit Reporting

Of course, if you default on your student loans the default will be reported to the major credit bureaus.[xiv] A default on your student loans will be harder to overcome when obtaining future credit than a bankruptcy.

## Default can Affect Your Employment

Beyond what your lender, the government, and the guarantor can do to you if you default, your employer may have an adverse reaction to wage garnishment. Wage garnishment creates extra paperwork, and therefore extra costs to your employer. If your employer is one who feels the extra costs are not worthwhile, then you may find yourself out of a job. Although it is not legal to fire someone because their wages are being garnished, or to refuse to hire someone for that reason, you may in fact find yourself unemployed, and without the option of an unemployment deferment.

Many employers consider a good credit rating a requirement for their employees. A history of paying your debts is considered to be an indication of good character. Some employers require a credit report prior to making an offer of employment, and when faced with a poor credit history they will select another prospective employee rather than take on someone who does not meet his or her obligations.

Interestingly enough, both the diamond industry and the lending industry use the magical 3Cs formula in business evaluation. In the diamond industry, each stone is evaluated for Carat, Color, and Clarity. In the lending industry, each potential borrower is evaluated for Character, Credentials, and Credit. A lender will check your good Character by contacting your references, your Credentials by your education and employment history, and your Credit by pulling a current credit report. A default on your student loans can mar all three of your Cs.

A student loan in deferment or forbearance shows up on your credit report as credit in good standing. Some employers, notably student loan lenders and guarantors, will discharge an employee for being delinquent on their student loan payments.

---

[xi] MPN

[xii] Kenneth R. Harney, "Sallie Mae agrees to report loan payment histories to credit bureaus", *Las Vegas Review-Journal and Las Vegas Sun*, p. 2F, (December 20, 2003).

[xiii] www.iowacollegeaid.org.

[xiv] http://www.tgslc.org/borrowers/whycare.cfm. TG is a federal loan guarantor.

[xv] http:/www.tgslc.org/borrowers/whycare.cfm.

[xvi] http://www.dlssonline.com This is the linked site to which I was directed from http://studentaid.ed.gov. This is actually the Direct Loans website, but the forms are applicable for Stafford loans as well.

# Chapter 4:  Deferments

*Pay now or Pay Later*

## Deferment is an Entitlement

Deferments are exactly what they sound like.  They defer (put off) payments on the loan(s) until a later time.  They are also an *entitlement*.  In simple language, if you meet the stated qualifications, you are entitled to the deferment and may not be denied.  This is the first major difference between deferment and forbearance.

In order to qualify for a deferment, you must meet all of the eligibility requirements, and your Master Promissory Note must have been signed during the year(s) in which the deferment has been allowed.  You must complete all required paperwork, and submit it to your lender.  You must complete the *most recent version* of the paperwork.  Since the deferment is offered by the government, and the requirements to qualify for the deferment are set by the government, the lender does not have the option of accepting incomplete, inaccurate, or outdated paperwork.

### The Government Pays the Interest

During deferment, the government will pay the interest on your *subsidized* loans.  This is the second major difference between deferment and forbearance.  The interest on *unsubsidized* and on private loans will accrue and capitalize, and will cause your loan balance to increase.  However, as mentioned in the section on interest, the interest on loans in deferment is lower than the interest on loans in repayment and in forbearance.  This is the third major difference between deferment and forbearance.

## There are Several Types of Deferments

There have been several different types of deferments available to student loan borrowers over the history of the program. Many of these deferment types are no longer extant. I will cover older loans in this chapter because your loan may be one of the older loans. I will pay more attention to the types of deferments available on the newer loans now being issued.

### Table 5: Possible Deferments

| Loan Type | In-School | Unemployment | Economic Hardship | Graduate Fellowship | Public Service | Parental |
|---|---|---|---|---|---|---|
| Stafford | Yes | Yes | Yes | Yes | Maybe | Maybe* |
| Direct | Yes | Yes | Yes | Yes | Maybe | Maybe* |
| Perkins | Yes | Yes | Yes | Yes | Yes | Maybe |
| PLUS | Maybe** | Yes | Yes | Maybe** | Maybe | No |
| SLS | Yes | Yes | Yes | Yes | Maybe | Maybe* |
| HEAL | Yes | Yes | Yes | Yes | ??? | ??? |
| Private | No*** | No*** | No*** | No*** | No*** | No*** |

In this next section, I will discuss the deferments available on Stafford, Direct, and PLUS loans. Perkins loan deferments will be covered in a separate section later in the chapter.

# In-School Deferments

> **Read this section. Some form of In-School Deferment applies to all federally guaranteed student loans. The limitations are important to you.**

The first and most popular type of deferment is the in-school deferment. There is no time limit on an in-school deferment. So long as the borrower is enrolled and attending school at an accredited institution of higher learning at least half time, the *borrower* can qualify for an in-school deferment on their federally guaranteed loans.

PLUS loans may be covered under in-school deferment, but **only** if the loan pre-dates 1986, **or** the parent borrower is now a student. During the financial aid application process, many people gain the impression all student loans qualify for in-school deferment. Later, many parent borrowers are stunned to discover they are delinquent on loans they believed they would not need to repay until after the student had graduated. If you came away from your financial aid interview with the belief that all student loans qualified for in-school deferment, you are not alone in your misconception. In fact, the rules changed and not everyone became aware of the changes.

---

**To qualify for an in-school deferment, the student/borrower must be enrolled in and attending classes *at least half-time*.**

---

Keep in mind, in order to qualify for the in-school deferment, the student/borrower must be enrolled and attending classes at least half time at an accredited institution of higher education, and the proper paperwork must be completed and submitted to the lender.

Your deferment may be revoked if you stop attending classes. If you take a semester off or change schools, the paperwork may not be filed in a timely fashion. It is the student's responsibility to see to it the school certifies his or her enrollment and attendance and communicates the information to the lender. After all, the student is the one who took out the loan, and it is the student who will benefit from the deferment. If you have any doubts about your status, contact your lender. The lender will make every effort to facilitate your deferment, but they can't do anything if they don't know what is going on.

---

**If your Master Promissory Note was signed after 1993, you may skip the next four deferments. They do not apply to you.**

---

# Education Related Deferments

Graduate Fellowship Deferment

For those of you fortunate enough to continue your education past your bachelor's degree in a Fellowship program, the government provides a Graduate Fellowship deferment. In order to qualify for graduate fellowship deferment you must hold at least a bachelor's degree, you must have been recommended to the program, and your status in the graduate fellowship program must be certified by an official of the program. The graduate Fellowship Deferment exists for those individuals pursuing graduate studies in a non-classroom environment. These individuals may be engaged in research, independent studies, or teaching assistant positions such that they fall below the required half-time classroom enrollment. They are, however, engaged in furthering their education on a full time basis. Like the in-school deferment, the graduate fellowship has no time limits so long as you are actively engaged in the fellowship program. Also, like the in-school deferment, the graduate fellowship deferment is available to the borrower on Stafford, Perkins, and Direct loans, or to the parent on a PLUS loan taken out *prior to 1993.*

Rehabilitation Training Deferment

Rehabilitation Training Programs qualify for a deferment. These may be programs designed to overcome physical or mental disabilities, or they may be drug or alcohol rehabilitation programs.

The program must be licensed or certified or in some manner approved and recognized by a state or federal agency and the Department of Education.

The program must provide individualized services to train and assist the individual in overcoming the limitations of his or her condition, and there must be a projected date at which the retraining will be completed.

The program must require a substantial time commitment. The individual involved must be unable to work or attend school full time as a result of their participation in the program.

The Rehabilitation Training Program deferment is available to the borrower on both Stafford and PLUS loans. It is available to the parent of the dependent student *only* on PLUS loans disbursed prior to 1993. The individual's participation in the program must be certified by an official of the program and by the borrower, and must include both beginning and ending dates for the program.

Internships and Residencies

Prior to 1993, the government allowed a deferment for internships and residencies. Prior to 1983, parent borrowers on PLUS loans qualified for the internships and residencies deferment. Between 1983 and 1993, only the student qualified. The program was designed to defer loan payments for health care professionals. It required the internship or residency to be conducted in a school, a hospital or a health care facility. It required a supervised training program, and the program had to require at least a bachelor's degree. There was a two year time limit on the deferment, and certification was required from the program official and the borrower, along with beginning and ending dates for the program. The internship and residency deferment is no longer available except to those borrowers whose loans were disbursed prior to 1993 (for student/borrowers only) or 1983 (for parent PLUS borrowers).

Teacher Shortage Deferment

Between 1987 and 1993, the government allowed a deferment for teachers who agreed to work in areas where teachers were in short supply. Teacher Shortage deferment was not available for PLUS loans. In order to qualify, the borrower must work full time as an elementary or secondary school teacher in a school or area on the identified Teacher Shortage Area list. The Teacher Shortage Area list is defined by the Department of Education on the recommendations of the chief state school official from each state. The teacher is required to re-apply and re-certify each year and the certification requires statements from both the borrower and the chief administrative officer of the school. The deferment has a maximum time limit of three years and is only available to borrowers whose loans were first disbursed between 1987 and 1993.

The In-School (*for PLUS borrowers only*), Graduate Fellowship, Rehabilitation Training, Internship/Residency/ and Teacher Shortage Area deferments are all covered by the Education Related Deferment form. You can obtain the most recent form at http://www.dlssonline.com/defer. This website is linked to the studentaid.ed.gov website.

## New Baby Deferments

**If your Master Promissory Note was signed after 1993, you may skip this section. New Baby Deferments do not apply to you.**

Parental Leave

Between 1987 and 1993, there was a Parental Leave Deferment. Parental leave deferment allowed a borrower who was pregnant or caring for a newborn or newly adopted child to take up to six months off from making payments. The qualifications for parental leave deferment are fairly complex.

The borrower must have been enrolled in school at least half time within the preceding six months, but not be currently enrolled in school. He or she must not be working full time (full time in this case being defined as thirty hours per week). There must, of course, be a child.

The borrower must be pregnant or caring for a newborn or newly adopted child. They must provide certification of their prior enrollment from the school, and a doctor's statement that they are pregnant or a copy of the child's birth certificate, or a statement from the adoption agency.

Parental leave deferment is only available to borrowers whose loans were first disbursed between 1987 and 1993.

Working Mother

Another in the series of 1987 through 1993 loan disbursement deferments is the Working Mother Deferment. Working mother deferment is relatively simple in its requirements. The working mother deferment applies only to the student/borrower and is not valid for parent loans.

The borrower must be female. She must have reentered the work force within the twelve months immediately preceding the deferment. She must have at least one child not yet enrolled in or beyond the first grade. She must be working full time, and earning no more than one dollar per hour over the current federal minimum wage.

The working mother deferment lasts for a period of twelve months and must be certified by the borrower with documentary proof of earnings (pay stubs) and of the existence of the pre-school aged child (birth certificate). Once again, the working mother deferment is only available on loans first disbursed between 1987 and 1993.

Both the Parental Leave and the Working Mother deferments use the same form. Go to http://www.dlssonline.com/defer to obtain the most up-to-date version.

## Public Service Deferments

Like most of the Education Related Deferments and the new baby deferments, the Public Service Deferments are only available for Stafford, PLUS, and Direct loans first disbursed prior to July 1993.

> **If your Master Promissory note was signed after 1993, you can skip this section. These deferments do not apply to you.**

## Armed Forces

The Armed Forces deferment is one of the career-related Public Service Deferments. Simply put, the borrower may defer his or her payments for a period of up to three years while serving on active duty in the United States Armed Forces, or while serving under an order for national mobilization. The three year limit for the Armed Forces deferment combines with a couple of other deferments (Public Health Service and NOAA) and is cumulative for all three deferments. In the unlikely event you qualify for all three deferments, (Armed Forces, NOAA, and Public Health Service), keep in mind the three year limit is *cumulative*. Certification comes from both the borrower and his or her commanding officer.

## Public Health Service

A full-time officer in the Commissioned Corps of Public Health of the United States Public Health Service may qualify for the same three years of deferment for Stafford or Direct loans disbursed under an MPN signed prior to 1993. He or she must be serving full time and certification is required from both the borrower and an authorized official from the Public Health Service. The three year cumulative time limit for deferment while an officer in the Public Health Services combines with the NOAA and Armed Forces deferments.

## NOAA

NOAA stands for National Oceanic and Atmospheric Administration Corps. Stafford loans disbursed between July of 1987 and June of 1993 may qualify for deferment. The borrower must be on active duty in the National Oceanic and Atmospheric Administration. Certification is by the borrower and an official of the National Oceanic and Atmospheric Administration, and the cumulative time limit of three years applies. The three year time limit for the NOAA deferment is cumulative for NOAA, Armed Forces and Public Health Services.

## Peace Corps

Borrowers who wish to join the Peace Corps may qualify for a deferment for up to three years. The Peace Corps deferment covers loans initially disbursed prior to 1983 (PLUS loans) or 1993 (Stafford loans), and the deferment applies to the borrower or the parents. In order to qualify, you must be serving in the Peace Corps full-time for a period of at least one year. Certification is by the borrower and an official of the Peace Corps.

## ACTION

The government will also allow you to defer your loans if you choose to serve as a domestic volunteer in an accredited ACTION program. The ACTION deferment covers loans initially disbursed prior to 1983 (PLUS loans) or 1993 (Stafford loans), and the deferment applies to the borrower or the parents. In order to qualify, you must be serving in the ACTION program full-time for a period of at least one year. Certification is by the borrower and an official of the ACTION program.

## Paid Full-Time Volunteers

The final career-based deferment is for full-time paid volunteers in tax-exempt organizations performing services comparable to Peace Corps or ACTION programs. Loans which qualify for paid volunteer deferment include: Stafford loans initially disbursed prior to July 1993, and PLUS loans disbursed prior to August 1983. To qualify for the volunteer deferment, you must be a full-time *paid* volunteer making no more than minimum wage. The program must provide service to low-income individuals and families, and be designed to help eliminate poverty and related conditions. Your service with the organization must be for a period of one year. You may not engage in religion-related activities as a part of your services. You may qualify for up to three years of deferment, depending upon the length of your service. Certification is by the borrower and an official of the program.

This ends the list of career-related deferments. All of these deferments use the Public Service deferment form. Please go to http://www.dlssonline.com/defer and obtain the most up-to-date version. This website also has instructions for completing the form.

## Temporary Disability Deferment

**If your Master Promissory Note was signed after 1993, you do not need to read this section. This deferment does not apply to you.**

The Temporary Total Disability Deferment is designed to relieve you of the responsibility of payments for a limited period of time when you are totally, but temporarily, disabled and unable to work. The *borrower* may defer payments for up to three years by re-certifying every six months. The temporary total disability deferment applies to Stafford, PLUS, SLS, and Consolidation loans disbursed prior to July 1993.

If the condition which causes the disability existed prior to obtaining the loan, then the condition must have *substantially* worsened since obtaining the loan. Also, keep in mind the temporary total disability is a temporary deferment for a *temporary* condition. The borrower must be unable to work or go to school full-time for a period of at least 60 days due to the disabling condition, *or* the borrower must be unable to work or go to school full-time for a period of at least 90 days because they are providing full-time care for a disabled dependent. A Complicated pregnancy may qualify for temporary total disability deferment. An uncomplicated pregnancy does not.

Your doctor must certify your condition and your inability to work full-time. If the condition persists beyond six months, it must be recertified in order to extend the deferment. There must be an anticipated recovery date.

If the condition is permanent and not expected to improve to the point where the borrower can return to work full-time, the temporary disability deferment does not apply. If the condition is permanent and not expected to improve, the appropriate action is to file for a discharge of the loan based upon the permanent and total disability. (*You may read more about permanent total disability in the chapter on discharges.*)

The applicable form may be obtained at http://www.dlssonline.com/defer.

As a reminder, most of the previously described deferments are available only on loans initially disbursed prior to July 1993, or in some cases earlier. Now I will move on to deferments available on more recently disbursed loans. (This completes the list of older deferments.)

## Unemployment Deferment

> **Read this section. All Stafford, Direct, and PLUS loans have some qualification for unemployment deferment.**

The first and most commonly used of the newer deferments is the Unemployment Deferment. You need not qualify for state unemployment benefits in order to qualify for the Unemployment Deferment.

In order to qualify for the unemployment deferment, the borrower must be substantially unemployed – that is he or she must be working less than 30 hours per week.

The borrower must be actively seeking full-time employment *in any field*. The key phrase there is *in any field*. Since the government may be paying a portion of the interest on your loans during deferment, they want to be sure you are actually looking for work. Despite the fact you now have a doctorate in rocket science, if the only jobs in your area are in food service, you should apply for a position in food service. Realistically, it is doubtful an employer will offer a job to an overqualified applicant no matter how often you apply, but go ahead and apply anyway. Being unemployed, as opposed to being independently wealthy and retired, isn't much fun anyway.

The borrower must register with an employment agency seeking permanent full-time work. This seems like a reasonable thing to do when you are looking for employment. If your community does not support a bricks and mortar employment agency, you may elect to use an on-line agency, such as Monster.com, or TrueCareers.com, or any of the other hundreds of on-line agencies, and if you are unemployed and actively seeking full-time work, you will no doubt post your resume with more than one of these agencies. According to the latest iteration of the Unemployment Deferment form, the first six months of deferment does not require documentation of your job search. However, if you need to extend the deferment for an additional six months, you will need to provide the information regarding your selected employment agency and the names of six different companies to whom you have applied for employment within the previous six months.

Unemployment deferments last for a period of six months and can be extended for up to three years, depending upon the age of the loan. For loans issued prior to July 1993, the cumulative limit of Unemployment deferment is two years (24 months) and for those issued after July 1993 the cumulative limit is three years (36 months). Therefore when your grace period runs out (assuming you never took a semester off and the grace period actually runs for the first six months after you graduate), if you don't have a job yet, you should apply for an unemployment deferment while you are seeking employment.

The Unemployment Deferment is available for Stafford loans, Perkins loans, Direct loans, and PLUS loans (so long as the *borrower* meets the qualifications).

Go to http://www.dlssonline.com/defer and obtain the most recent Stafford/Direct form, along with instructions. Perkins loan deferments are all covered on a single form. Contact your school or servicing agency for the latest Perkins form.

## Economic Hardship Deferment

**If your Master Promissory Note was signed before 1993, you may skip this section. Your loan does not qualify for this deferment.**

The Economic Hardship Deferment takes the place of all those various career-related, education related (except for the Graduate Fellowship) new baby-related deferments and the Temporary Disability Deferment. Economic Hardship deferment is only available on loans issued *after July 1993*. Economic Hardship deferment is a catch-all deferment designed to provide relief for borrowers who are not in a position to make payments, but who do not qualify for an Unemployment Deferment. The Economic Hardship deferment is also the most complex of the deferments for which to qualify. The borrower must meet at least one of the following criteria. He or she must:

*Requirement:* Have already qualified for an Economic Hardship Deferment under the Perkins loan programs for the same period of time for which he/she is applying for deferment on his/her Stafford, Direct, SLS, PLUS or Consolidated loans

*Solution:* If you have already filled out the worksheet and qualified for the same Deferment on your Perkins loans, you need not do it all again. Simply provide evidence you have qualified and are receiving the Perkins Deferment.

**or**

*Requirement:* Be eligible for and receiving federal or state public assistance in the form of food stamps, Aid to Families with Dependent Children (AFDC), Supplemental Security Income (SSI) or another authorized program

*Solution:* Provide copies of the award letters granting federal or state public assistance. These award letters *must* be current. Your local welfare department will be happy to assist you in this matter.

**or**

*Requirement:* Be working full-time but earning no more than federal minimum wage or the poverty level for a family of two

*Solution:* You will need to provide copies of the most recent 30 days of pay stubs.

**or**

*Requirement:* Be working full-time but have a federal education debt burden exceeding 20% of gross income *and* income minus debt service must be less than 220% of the greater of minimum wage or the poverty level for a family of two

*Solution:* You will need to provide copies of the most recent 30 days of pay stubs and documentation of the most recent payments due on all federal education loans.

**or**

*Requirement:* Not be working full-time and earning a gross monthly income not to exceed twice the greater amount of minimum wage or the poverty level for a family of two *and* income minus federal education debt service cannot exceed the greater of minimum wage or the poverty level for a family of two.

*Solution:* Certification may include a copy of the most recent tax return (only if filed within the last 8 months), copies of the most recent 30 days of pay-stubs, and documentation of the most recent payments due on all federal education loans. However, if you have no income – no earnings, no AFDC, no Food Stamps, no trust fund, no nothing (you are a stay-at-home parent, perhaps) – then you simply state, "I have zero income," and ignore the rest of the calculations.

Interestingly enough, although the directions for this deferment make no reference to the Peace Corps, Item 3 of Section 2 of the official form lists volunteering in the Peace Corps as one of the qualifying conditions. So, if you are a Peace Corps volunteer (for a full year), this deferment takes the place of the Public Service Deferment for loans initiated after 1993.

As you can see, determining eligibility for an economic hardship deferment will be a relatively complex calculation. Certification includes a copy of the most recent tax return (but only if filed within the last 8 months), copies of the most recent 30 days of pay stubs, copies of the award letters granting federal or state public assistance, and documentation of the most recent payments due on all federal education loans.

As challenging as qualifying for an economic hardship deferment may be, it is frequently the best way for a borrower to manage his or her educational loans. The economic hardship deferment may be available for two or three years (in one year increments, depending on when your loan was initiated) on Stafford, Perkins, Direct loans, and on PLUS loans.

Perkins deferment forms can be obtained at the school from which you received the loan or go to http://www.dlssonline.com/defer for the Stafford/Direct/PLUS form.

**Poverty Levels**

For informational purposes, the federal government calculates the poverty level each year, and makes the figures available on a website located at www.ocpp.org/poverty/index.htm.  Since this information may not be at your fingertips, I am reproducing the figures for 2004 here.  You can check the government website for updated information.  Keep in mind although the federal government calculates poverty levels for all family sizes, the deferment specifically cites poverty level for a *family of two*.

## Table 6:  2004 Poverty Levels

| Number in Family | Gross Yearly Income | Gross Monthly Income | Approximate Hourly Income |
|---|---|---|---|
| 1 | $ 9,310 | $ 776 | $ 4.48 |
| **2** | **12,490** | **1,041** | **6.00** |
| 3 | 15,670 | 1,306 | 7.53 |
| 4 | 18,850 | 1,571 | 9.06 |
| 5 | 22,030 | 1,836 | 10.59 |
| 6 | 25,210 | 2,101 | 12.12 |
| 7 | 28,390 | 2,366 | 13.65 |
| 8 | 31,570 | 2,631 | 15.18 |
| Over 8 in family, add for each person | + 3,180 | + 265 | + 1.53 |

Table 7 below should simplify the deferments available on Stafford, SLS, Direct, and PLUS loans.

## Table 7: Stafford, Direct, SLS, PLUS Deferments

| Form | Deferment Type | Time Limit | Stafford, SLS, Direct Loans | | | PLUS Loans | | |
|------|----------------|------------|-----|-----|-----|-----|-----|-----|
| | | | Pre 1987 | 7/87 to 6/93 | 7/93 to present | Pre-1983 | 7/87 to 6/93 | 7/93 to present |
| SCH | In-school full-time | None | Yes | Yes | Yes | Yes[*] | Yes[*] | Yes[**] |
| | In-school half-time | None | | Yes | Yes | | Yes[*] | Yes[**] |
| EDU | Graduate fellowship | None | Yes | Yes | Yes | Yes[**] | Yes[**] | Yes[**] |
| | Rehabilitation training | None | Yes | Yes | Yes | Yes[**] | Yes[**] | Yes[**] |
| PUB | Military or Public Health Service | 3 yrs | Yes | Yes | No | Yes | No | No |
| | NOAA | 3 yrs | No | Yes | No | No | No | No |
| | Pease Corps/ Domestic/ Tax-Exempt org. | 3 yrs | Yes | Yes | No | Yes | No | No |
| EDU | Teacher shortage | 3 yrs | No | Yes | No | No | No | No |
| | Internship/Residency | 2 yrs | Yes | Yes | No | Yes | No | No |
| DIS | Temporary Total Disability | 3 yrs | Yes | Yes | No | Yes | Yes | Yes |
| UNEM | Unemployment | 2 yrs | Yes | Yes | | Yes | Yes | Yes |
| | | 3 yrs | | | Yes | | | |
| FAM | Parental Leave | 6 mo | Yes | Yes | No | No | No | No |
| | Working Mother | 1 yr | No | Yes | No | No | No | No |
| EHD | Economic Hardship | 3 yrs | No | No | Yes | No | No | Yes |

# Perkins Loans Deferments

Perkins loan deferments are a group of deferments available *only* to Perkins loan borrowers. Perkins loan deferments are, in many cases, precursors to actual loan discharge, and are available to borrowers serving in designated public service positions.

Perkins loan deferments are not available on Stafford, Direct, or PLUS loans, although forbearance may be available for individuals serving in the same capacities. Perkins loan deferments available include:

- **Teacher**: A full-time teacher (elementary or secondary) serving students from low-income families. The school must be on the designated list. Qualifies for deferment, *may also qualify for 100% discharge.*
- **Teacher, Special Education**: A full-time special education teacher (elementary or secondary) serving special needs children. Qualifies for deferment, *may also qualify for 100% discharge.*
- **Early Intervention Services for the Disabled**: A full-time qualified provider of early intervention services for the disabled. Qualifies for deferment, *may also qualify for 100% discharge.*
- **Teacher, Math, Science, Languages, or Teacher Shortage Area**: A full-time teacher of math, science, foreign languages, bilingual languages or any other field designated as a teacher shortage area. Qualifies for deferment, *may also qualify for 100% discharge.*
- **Public or Non-profit Family Services**: A full-time employee of a public or non-profit child or family services agency providing services to high-risk children and their families in low-income neighborhoods. Qualifies for deferment, *may also qualify for 100% discharge.*
- **Nurse or Medical Technician**: A full-time nurse or medical technician qualifies for deferment, *may also qualify for 100% discharge.*
- **Nurse**: Available through the U.S. Department of Health and Human Services' Nurses Education Loan Repayment Program (NERLP), a registered nurse's loans may be repaid in exchange for service in eligible facilities. *Full-time service for two years will repay 60% of a participant's qualifying loan balance, three years full-time service will repay 85%.* Go to www.bhpr.hrsa.gov/nursing/loanrepay.htm.
- **Law Enforcement or Corrections Officer**: A full-time law enforcement or corrections officer may qualify for deferment *and for 100% discharge.*
- **Head Start Program**: A full-time member of the education component of the Head Start program may qualify for deferment *and for 100% discharge.*
- **Vista or Peace Corps:** A Vista or Peace Corps volunteer may qualify for deferment *and for up to 70% discharge.*
- **U. S. Armed Forces**: An individual serving in the U.S. Armed Forces may qualify for deferment and up to 50% discharge if serving in *hostile action* or in *imminent danger.*

As of October 7, 1998, all Perkins loans are eligible for the above discharge benefits regardless of when the loan was made. The benefit is *not* retroactive to services performed prior to October 7, 1998.

Also available to Perkins borrowers are the same deferments available to newer Stafford and Direct Loan borrowers. Unemployment, Economic Hardship, In-school (at least half-time) and Graduate fellowship program deferments are available. Interestingly enough, most Perkins deferments are accomplished on a single form. You fill out the top portion and check the box which applies. You *do* have to provide supporting documentation. The requirements for the Economic Hardship Deferment are the same for Perkins and Stafford/Direct loan borrowers.

Contact your school or loan servicing agency for the proper paperwork. Now that you have read through all of the various types of deferments, it should be clear there are at most 60 months of deferment time available to most borrowers. Hopefully you won't need to use all or even any of those months. However, if you are unable to make your payments for any reason, I would encourage you to explore the deferment options thoroughly before going on to forbearance.

---

* Yes if first loan was disbursed prior to 1993, otherwise No.
** Yes if first loan was disbursed prior to 1986 or if borrower is **now** a student.
*** Lender may allow deferral of payments
* parent borrower or student meets requirements
** parent borrower meets requirements

# Chapter 5:  Forbearance

*Pay now or pay LOTS More later*

Forbearance is the lender's permission to delay payments or to make smaller than normally scheduled payments.  The effect of forbearance is similar to deferment – you are allowed to put off your payments.  However, during forbearance the government does not participate in any way in the payment of your interest.  *All interest due during forbearance must be paid by the borrower or it will be capitalized.*  I discussed interest and capitalization in the Introduction.

Forbearance is generally optional on the part of the lender.  Lenders' policies regarding forbearance vary widely.  Some lenders allow up to five years (60 months) of forbearance and grant it simply for the asking.  Others allow only two years (24 months).  Many lenders require the borrower to qualify for forbearance under their policy guidelines.  Some will grant the first two years with no questions, and require proof of need in order to obtain additional forbearance time.  Perkins loans have a maximum of three years (36 months) and require income qualification similar to the Economic Hardship Deferment.

Forbearance policies change from time to time.  As of this writing, many of the national student loan lenders (Stafford and PLUS loans) will grant forbearance over the telephone, with no paperwork involved.  Others require the paperwork to be completed and mailed (not faxed) to their office.  Many lenders will allow forms to be completed and filed on-line.

No book can adequately inform you of your lender's policies since those policies vary from lender to lender and are subject to change at any given time, so you must keep in contact with your lender.  If you have questions about the amount of time available to you, or the policies your lender currently uses, call them on their toll-free number or check out their web-site for up-to-date information.

An added word of advice; call Tuesday through Thursday.  Mondays are the highest call-volume days for most lenders and on Fridays people are getting ready for the weekend. You will get the best service, and experience the shortest wait-times by calling midweek.

## Discretionary Forbearance

There are actually several types of forbearance available. Your concern may be primarily with discretionary forbearance. Discretionary forbearance is offered by the lender to assist you at times when you really cannot make your payments, but you don't qualify for any deferments. Inability to make your payments may be because of unusual expenses in your life, or because of health issues which keep you from working full-time but do not qualify you for disability deferment. Many times, home mortgage lenders will advise borrowers to place their student loans into voluntary (discretionary) forbearance in order to qualify for a higher home mortgage payment, and most student loan lenders (Stafford and PLUS loans) will allow this use of discretionary forbearance. Having already read the section on interest, you understand how dangerous using forbearance can be for you financially.

## Administrative Forbearance

A second type of forbearance available is the administrative forbearance. Administrative forbearance is applied by the lender on a limited basis. For example, many lenders will apply an administrative forbearance (even when the borrower has no discretionary forbearance time left to them) to a delinquent account if the borrower signs up for automatic payments from their checking account. Not all lenders will accept automatic payments from checking accounts, not all will grant administrative forbearance to clear up a delinquency when setting up automatic payments, and those who do will frequently limit the forbearance time granted in this manner to only a few months. Check with your lender to learn their specific policy.

# Mandatory Forbearance

There is also a mandatory forbearance. The term mandatory refers to the lender, not the borrower. During the most recent (2003) Gulf War conflict, for example, the government determined the troops being sent overseas should be temporarily relieved of some of their financial burdens.[xvii] Deferments are entitlements and require the government to participate in the cost of interest on subsidized loans. Deferments, therefore, require congressional funding and budgeting. However, forbearances don't cost the government anything. The Department of Education requires all lenders make available to mobilized borrowers a special military forbearance for the period of their deployment. The borrower has the option of taking advantage of this forbearance or not – the lender has no choice in the matter.

Other circumstances which currently require your lender to grant you forbearance include:[xviii]

- serving in an internship or residency program, if the program is approved and you meet program requirements, (This replaces the internship deferment no longer available.)
- serving in a national service position for which you receive a national educational award (reviewed later in Chapter 6 Loan Discharges), (Replacing the public service deferment.)
- qualifying for partial repayment under the Student Loan Repayment program administered by the Department of Defense (also mentioned later), (Replacing the Armed Forces deferment.)
- qualifying for loan forgiveness under the Teacher Loan Forgiveness program (up to five years, see Chapter 6 Loan Discharges), (Replacing the Teacher Shortage deferment.)
- qualifying for loan forgiveness under the Child Care Provider loan forgiveness program (up to five years, see Chapter 6 Loan Discharges), and
- qualifying for economic hardship forbearance available under Title IV. The Economic Hardship Forbearance (also called Title IV forbearance) is designed to provide relief for borrowers whose loans pre-date the Economic Hardship Deferment, but who do not qualify for any of the career-related deferments or the Temporary Disability Deferment. An

economic hardship forbearance may provide up to three additional years of forbearance time to a borrower. The economic hardship forbearance requires the monthly debt burden for Title IV loans must equal or exceed 20% of the borrower's gross monthly income or the borrower must meet one of the other qualifying requirements for the economic hardship deferment.

Mandatory Forbearance is mandatory on the part of the lender however, with the exception of the previously mentioned 'Gulf War' forbearance and Title IV Economic Hardship Forbearance, it *does* count against your forbearance time.

## Mandatory Administrative Forbearance

Mandatory Administrative forbearance is similar in nature to a mandatory forbearance. In the aftermath of 9/11, a mandatory administrative forbearance was applied to all student loans in the New York City area (or so I was told when I worked at SallieMae). In this case, the interest was suspended as well. Because of the unusual circumstances, the suspension of interest and payments was considered to be in the nation's best interests. No one knew for many days whether certain borrowers were even alive, and those who were alive might have been unable to work due to the destruction of their workplace or the transportation issues which arose. Clearly the mandatory administrative forbearance is not used often.

## Perkins Loan Forbearance

Perkins Loans may also qualify for discretionary forbearance, but it isn't the sort of thing you can do over the telephone the way you may be able to with Stafford loans. The necessary form can be obtained from your school. You will discover that in order to qualify for forbearance on a Perkins Loan, you must provide income and expense information. You have a maximum of three years (not five) of discretionary forbearance time available to you, and you must agree to payment arrangements for the interest which accrues during forbearance. Of course this forces you to deal with the accruing interest, so it doesn't grow uncontrolled.

To summarize, a borrower may have *up to* five years of discretionary forbearance time available. Borrowers who would qualify for the Economic Hardship Deferment under the basis of need, but whose loans were issued prior to 1993 may qualify for an additional three years of economic hardship forbearance time (mandatory forbearance). During forbearance, all interest accrues. If not paid by the borrower, interest is capitalized and added to the balance of the loan. The loan balance goes up. The payment goes up because the loan balance has gone up. Once the interest is capitalized, the lender charges interest on the interest. Any time you feel the need to place your loans into discretionary forbearance, first go back and re-read the section on interest. Then you can make an informed decision.

---

[xvii] http://studentaid.ed.gov/students/publications
[xviii] Master Promissory Note

# Chapter 6:  Loan Discharges

*Get rid of some or all*

Basically, there are three ways to get out from under your student loan debt. The easiest way is to pay them.  The second easiest way is to die.  The third way is to qualify for one of the loan discharge or partial discharge programs.

The Department of Education changes forms regularly, and only the newest and most current are acceptable so I have not included copies of the forms.  I have described the requirements necessary to qualify for discharge.  If you believe you qualify for a loan discharge or partial discharge, contact your lender for the most current paperwork, or go to http://studentaid.ed.gov/students/publications and follow the prompts for the latest Stafford, Direct, and PLUS forms, or contact your school for Perkins forms.

## Death

The death of a borrower discharges his or her student loan obligation.  The death of the student discharges the obligation of the parent borrower on a PLUS loan.  On the bright side, there are no "Death Discharge" forms to be completed, but the lender does need *an original copy of the death certificate.*

In the interests of minimizing the pain for your surviving relatives should you pass into the great beyond, you need to keep all of your student loan documentation together.  A lender does not know a borrower has died until someone informs them of that fact.  Then the lender requires a copy of the borrower's death certificate in order to cease collection efforts.

As a former default prevention specialist, it was my duty to call on delinquent loans.  Normally, I was able to offer meaningful assistance in clearing up the financial problems.  But the hardest and saddest call of all was the one to a surviving parent, spouse or child.  The collector usually reaches the surviving family member about three months after the death, when they are just beginning to be able to put the horror aside and get on with the business of living.

The mother, or wife or husband or child receives a phone call asking for their missing loved one. "He died," they say, with tears in their voice. More than anything, at this point I wanted to simply express my heartfelt condolences and end the call, but if I did that, someone else would have to call back. So I had to ask, 'when'. And I had to ask, 'where'. And I had to ask for a copy of the death certificate. 'An original, please – with the seal.'

All of this is very hard on the surviving family members. Of course, you won't be there to suffer along with them, but try to think about the ramifications of your possible death ahead of time.

## Disability

A third way to discharge a student loan is to become 100%, totally and permanently disabled. While working in default prevention, I used to tell people, "If you are lying in the hospital, in a coma, not expected to recover, some doctor will come along and say, 'Well, but he might come out of it,' and there goes your disability discharge." Doctors do not like to declare a person hopeless for recovery. A doctor will typically declare you 80% disabled, or 50%, or anything other than 100%. Typically, a doctor will waffle like a politician about the possibility of recovery.

With new research going on all the time, and new treatments for old conditions, it is very difficult for any doctor to state a person will never recover. *Total and permanent disability is defined as the inability to work and earn money because of an illness or injury which is expected to continue indefinitely or to result in death.* Total and permanent disability is the condition which the government requires in order to discharge a loan for disability.

### Step One: the Paperwork

The paperwork must be completed in its entirety. Take a good look at the disability discharge form. It looks really simple, and the paperwork reduction notice says the form should take no more than 30 minutes to complete. This is very true, as far as it goes, but the accompanying documentation is another matter. If there is a space on page one for the doctor's license number, and a similar space on page two, but no such space appears on page three, and the space occurs again on page four, then all blanks must be completed. If there is a place to enter a date on line one and the same date applies to the blank on line six, the same date must be entered on both lines. Doctors don't seem to like filling out redundant information – particularly when the redundancy occurs within the same paragraph. If your doctor leaves anything blank, or unclear, or if his handwriting is illegible, the form will be returned to you.

In any event, if you simply have your doctor complete the form and send it in without supporting documentation, you will be performing …

## Step Two: the Paperwork

Everything your doctor filled out in Step One must be done over again. He may not use white-out to make corrections. He may not cross through and make corrections. He may not send additional documentation under separate cover. All the paperwork together now, and in one envelope. All accompanying documentation must contain all of your doctor's information – name, license number, state of licensing – and the diagnosis must remain the same from one page to the next and from one submission to the next.

## Step Three: the Paperwork

It may seem to you as if your lender is being unreasonably fussy. However, your lender only reviews the documentation. The Department of Education makes the final decision, and your lender has had too many claims rejected due to missing or incomplete paperwork. You must send original documents. No facsimile copies will be accepted. Original signatures are required on all paperwork.

## Step Four: Waiting

You will probably need to submit complete documentation to your lender at least three times before it gets to the Department of Education (DoE) for review, and there is a good chance something will be lost along the way and have to be provided yet again. Once the Department of Education has your paperwork, they must review the case. This is not a quick and easy process, so be patient.

Be prepared to make payments during the process or to receive calls from your lender and/or the guarantor and/or a collection agency. If you are receiving collection calls from the guarantor's office, you may be offered the option of placing the loan into forbearance while you wait for your disability discharge to be processed. Just as a minor warning, when you place your loans in forbearance, you state or claim in writing your intention to repay the loan upon expiration of the forbearance. If you claim intention to repay the loan while you are in the process of trying to have the loan discharged, you could open yourself up to a charge of lender fraud. On the other hand, your lender may *advise* you to accept forbearance. Consult with your own legal advisors before making this decision. Neither the author nor the publisher is qualified to advise you on this matter.

## Step Five: You're Approved

When your request for discharge of a student loan due to disability is approved, *keep the paperwork*. Set up a permanent file for student loan papers, and file the letter showing your loan has been discharged. (A permanent file is also recommended for the paid-in-full letter you receive when you pay off a loan.)

Lenders sell loans, and they usually sell bundles of loans. Neither the selling lender nor the purchasing lender examines each loan package individually to determine whether or not the loan is still valid. Although I have never personally made collection calls on loans discharged through disability, I have talked with borrowers who were wise enough to keep their paid-in-full letters. Having the paid-in-full letter on file means you can simply fax a copy to that annoying collector and be done with it.

You also need to know your discharge is *conditional*.[xix] Since July 1, 2002, a borrower who has had his or her loans discharged due to total and permanent disability is conditionally released for a period of three years from the date of total and permanent disability. During this three year period, the borrower is not required to pay principal or interest on the loan(s). They are, however, required to recertify their ongoing disability. After this time, if the borrower continues to meet the requirements of total and permanent disability, the loan is canceled. If the borrower does not continue to meet the requirements for total and permanent disability, they must resume payments on the loan.

> Since July 1, 2002, a borrower who applies for and receives a discharge on their student loans due to total and permanent disability may be ***conditionally released*** for a period of three years. After three years, if the borrower continues to meet the requirements of total and permanent disability, the loan is cancelled. ***If the borrower does not meet the conditions for total and permanent disability, they must resume payments on the loan***.

### Beyond the Paperwork

If you were disabled at the time you received your student loans, and you are requesting discharge of those debts based on the same disability, your condition must have *substantially worsened* in the intervening years.

## Partial Discharge of Teacher's Stafford Loans

Partial discharge of teacher's student loans has been available from time to time throughout the history of the student loan program. Teachers are vital to our national economy and our national defense. Unfortunately, teachers are some of the poorest paid professionals in our society. I have a very clear memory from my youth of former Governor Jerry Brown of California in a public speech saying low salaries for teachers and civil servants were appropriate because teachers receive 'psychic pay' in excess of their monetary remuneration. At the time, his statement caused a great deal of furor among teachers and other public employees. We can only hope they *do* receive psychic pay since we certainly don't pay them a monetary wage commensurate with their training and education and the influence they have on our young people. The federal government does have a current program designed to partially forgive teacher's Stafford and Direct loans. Under this partial forgiveness program a teacher may have up to $5,000 of federal student loans forgiven if:[xx]

- He or she borrowed a Stafford Loan through the Federal Family Education Loan (FFEL) and/or Federal Direct Loan program, *and*
- He or she had no outstanding FFEL or Direct Loan balances on October 1, 1998, *or*
- He or she paid off the outstanding balance on his or her FFEL or Direct loans before obtaining the loan for which they are requesting forgiveness, *and*

> **No Stafford or Direct Loans older than 1998. If you had them, you must have paid them off and obtained new loans after 1998.**

- He or she has been employed for at least five consecutive school years as a full-time elementary or secondary school teacher in either a public or private (non-profit) school *designated as a low-income school, **and***
- At least one of these consecutive years occurred after the 1997-98 academic year.

> **Five years of qualified teaching, at least one of them after 1998.**

Please note, the partial discharge requires that you teach for five years. Service as an administrator at the school does not qualify you for the partial discharge.

There are three exceptions to the 'consecutive years' requirement.
- The borrower was called to active duty military for more than 30 days, *or*
- The borrower has a condition covered by the Family Medical Leave Act, *or*
- The borrower returned to postsecondary education for a purpose related to performing the teaching service for which they are requesting forgiveness (back to school for a Master's Degree or additional certificate).

In order for any of these exceptions to be allowed, the borrower must have taught for at least one-half of an academic term and the employer (school or school district) must consider the borrower to have fulfilled their contract terms for the purposes of salary increases, tenure, and retirement.

- The borrower may not be in default on the FFEL or Direct Loan for which they are requesting forgiveness, or if in default they must have established a satisfactory repayment arrangement with their lender, *and*
- The borrower may not have received a benefit for the same teaching service under the National and Community Service Act of 1990 (Americorps), *and*
- The loan for which forgiveness is requested must have been issued prior to the end of the fifth year of qualifying teaching, *and*
- For elementary school teachers, the school's chief administrative officer must certify the borrower demonstrates knowledge and teaching skills in certain areas of the elementary school curriculum, *or*
- For secondary school teachers, the school's chief administrative officer must certify the borrower teaches in a subject area relevant to his/her academic major.

When requesting forgiveness of loans, the borrower should include all relevant documentation, including the certification from the school's chief administrative officer. Due to the time involved in reviewing and processing requests for forgiveness, the borrower must either continue to make the necessary payments on the loans, or arrange with the lender for forbearance.

# School Related Discharges of Stafford, Direct, and PLUS loans[xxi]

### School Closure

From time to time schools close without warning. Students who have obtained loans to attend those schools, but not yet completed their course of study may be able to have their debt discharged. Discharge of student loans because of school closure is not an automatic occurrence. Sometimes the school makes arrangements for the student to complete the term at another, nearby facility. Sometimes the school simply closes and the funds disappear.

If you find yourself in this circumstance, contact your lender *immediately*. Your lender will take down the necessary information and provide you with the appropriate paperwork to have the loan discharged. Unless you complete the proper paperwork, this loan will come back to haunt you at some future date.

When you receive the discharge paperwork, file it carefully with all the data relevant to the discharged loan. Loans may be 100% discharged due to school closure if received on or after January 1, 1986. Be advised if arrangements are made by the school to have you continue through certification at another school, the loans may not qualify for discharge. If you are allowed to transfer your education credits to another school, the loans may not qualify for discharge or may be only partially dischargeable. The idea is you should not be damaged by a school closure – pay for something you did not receive – but you should still pay for that which you did receive.

## False Certification (Ability to Benefit)

If your school admitted you without proper testing or documentation (high school diploma, GED, test scores, etc.) that you have the ability to learn and benefit from education, you may be able to have the loan discharged. An extreme example might include an individual who has reached the age of majority but remains in guardianship. Such a person is not competent to contract for a loan. A profoundly retarded individual admitted into a standard college program might also qualify.

## False Certification (Disqualifying Status)

In order to qualify for False Certification (Disqualifying Status), you must have been unable to meet the legal requirements of your state of residence to serve in the profession or position for which the program would train you. For PLUS loans, this would be the state of residence of the student for whose benefit the loan was obtained. Generally, the legal requirements will be related to age, physical or mental condition, or criminal record. If you have a criminal conviction for drug trafficking or child molestation, you may be unable to obtain state licensing as a teacher.  But if you do not disclose the facts on your application for admission, the school may certify you anyway.  If false certification occurs because of your omissions or misrepresentations, you are unlikely to obtain a discharge of the loan(s).  If you are 70 years old at the time you enter a criminal justice course of study, you may be unable to meet state age requirements for police work.

## Unauthorized Signature/Unauthorized Payment

Unauthorized Signature/Unauthorized Payment discharge covers loans or disbursements obtained through forgery.  Occasionally, someone in the financial aid office will divert funds that should have gone to a student's account and take those funds for personal use.  Although this is a very rare occurrence, the government makes provision for the discharge of loans which were fraudulently diverted.

From time to time students have been known to forge a parent's or grandparent's signature on a loan application.  Obviously, if you did not sign the MPN, you are not liable for the loan.  However, your lender and the government want to be sure they aren't discharging valid loans.  They require signature samples for comparison.  And you can be assured the person who forged your signature will be subject to criminal charges.

## Unpaid Refund

Some schools are unable to process refunds.  When the school has already received the funds for a student, but the student – for whatever reason – is unable to attend classes for that semester, the funds must be returned.  In most cases, the school simply returns the funds to the lender.  If the school is unable to return the funds to the lender then the student must apply for an Unpaid Refund discharge.

Your lender can provide you with the most current forms, or you can go to studentaid.ed.gov/publications/student.  Perkins borrowers must contact their school.

# Stafford, Direct, and PLUS Partial Payments

### Military Service

From time to time, the Armed Forces will offer partial repayment of student loans as an enlistment inducement. It is important to note that an offer of partial repayment is not a discharge or forgiveness of the loan. After serving the specified amount of time in the Armed Forces, the Secretary of Defense will make a lump-sum payment to your lender. However, until the Secretary of Defense actually makes the payment, you are still responsible for payments on your loan. Many military personnel use forbearance to manage their cash flow issue by placing their loans in forbearance for one year. At the end of that year, if the paperwork is completed in a timely fashion, the Secretary of Defense sends a check to the borrower's lender. This forbearance cycle can be repeated for up to five years, depending upon the amount the military agreed to pay on behalf of the recruit and the amount of discretionary forbearance time the borrower's lender allows.

### Community Service Educational Awards

Volunteers who serve in an approved national or community service program (such as Americorps) may earn an educational award. An educational award can be used to pay your Stafford loans. The borrower must either place his or her loans in forbearance while performing this service, or he or she must keep the payments current. The educational award will be distributed at the end of the year of service. Be careful not to go into default while waiting for your administrator to pay your loan for you.

# Full-time Child Care Provider[xxii]

A borrower who has a degree in early childhood education, is a full-time child care provider and who had no outstanding balance on a Stafford loan or a Direct loan on October 7, 1998, or who had no outstanding balance on a FFELP loan on the date they obtained a loan after October 7, 1998 (they had a balance, but paid it off prior to obtaining the new loan after October 7, 1998), may qualify for loan forgiveness under a demonstration program set forth in the Higher Education Act of 1965 as amended and applicable under Department of Education regulations.

In order to qualify[xxiii] for the full-time child care provider discharge, you must be a new borrower in accordance with the dates set forth above. You must have obtained a degree in early childhood education from an institution of higher education. If you received a degree in another field of study, and later obtained a degree in early childhood education, a maximum of two years of funding may be eligible for forgiveness.

The families for whom you are providing child care services must meet income guidelines, and those guidelines vary by state. 70% of the children receiving child care at the facility at which you work must be from families whose incomes are not more than 85% of the State median income.

You must work full-time, 12 months per year, for two consecutive years in order to qualify for 20% forgiveness on your qualifying loans. After the third year, you may qualify for an additional 20% forgiveness, and after the fourth and fifth years, you may qualify for 30% forgiveness for each of those years.

You may not receive an education award for any of those years of service under the National Community Service Act of 1990 (Americorps). The full-time child care provider program may qualify you for a mandatory forbearance while providing the child care services, and for discharge of your loans.

This program requires annual funding and those funds cannot possibly go as far as we would all like them to. Funds may not be available when you wish to apply for forgiveness. Call 1-888-562-7002 for the necessary forms.

Table 8 summarizes discharges. Refer to the text for the requirements and conditions of each type.

## Table 8: Discharge options

| Reason for Discharge | Stafford | Direct | Perkins | PLUS | Student PLUS/SLS | HEAL |
|---|---|---|---|---|---|---|
| Death | Yes | Yes | Yes | Yes* | Yes | Yes |
| Disability# | Yes | Yes | Yes | Yes+ | Yes | Yes |
| School Closure** | Yes | Yes | Yes | Yes | Yes | Yes |
| False Certification/Ability to Benefit | Yes | Yes | Yes | Yes | Yes | Yes |
| False Certification/Disqualifying Status | Yes | Yes | Yes | Yes | Yes | Yes |
| Unauthorized Signature | Yes | Yes | Yes | Yes | Yes | Yes |
| Unpaid Refund | Yes | Yes | Yes | Yes | Yes | Yes |
| Teaching | Maybe## | Maybe## | Yes | No | No | No |
| Military | Maybe++ | Maybe++ | Yes | No | No | No |
| Community Service/Educational Award | Maybe*** | Maybe*** | Yes | No | No | No |
| Full-time Child Care Provider | Maybe+++ | Maybe+++ | No | No | No | No |
| Nursing | No | No | Yes | No | No | Maybe |
| Law Enforcement/Corrections | No | No | Yes | No | No | No |
| Bankruptcy√ | Maybe | Maybe | Maybe | Maybe | Maybe | Maybe |

# Perkins Loan Discharge Programs[xxiv]

## Perkins Loan Discharge of Teacher's Loans

The Perkins Loan Program for discharge of teacher's loans is much more liberal than the Stafford loan program. As mentioned in the deferment section, a full-time teacher's Perkins loans may be eligible for 100% discharge if the teacher is

- A full-time teacher in a designated school serving students from low-income families,

- A full-time special education teacher,
- A full-time teacher of math, science, foreign languages, bilingual education, or another field designated as a teacher shortage area, or
- A full-time member of the education component of the Head Start Program.

These loans may also be eligible for deferment while the teacher is performing his or her teaching duties to qualify for the discharge. Forms for deferment and discharge are available from the school from which you obtained your loan.

## Military Service

As mentioned in the chapter on deferments, Perkins Loans may qualify for *up to* 50% forgiveness/discharge for military personnel serving in areas of hostilities or imminent danger. Forms are available from your school for deferment or discharge of Perkins loans.

## Community Service

The Perkins Loan discharge Programs are more generous for those in community service than the Stafford, and Direct programs.

Vista and Peace Corps volunteers may qualify for up to 70% loan discharge, and they may be eligible for deferment while serving.

Full-time employees of public or non-profit child or family services agencies providing services to high-risk children and their families may be eligible for 100% discharge, and may qualify for deferment while performing these services. This discharge correlates to a deferment no longer available on Stafford loans (except older Stafford loans). Early intervention specialists serving the disabled community may also qualify for 100% discharge and deferment.

## Nursing

As mentioned earlier, Perkins Loan borrowers may qualify for up to 100% discharge of their eligible loans when serving as a full-time nurse or medical technician.

There is also the NELRP nursing program which is not a discharge, but a payment of your loan by a third party after serving for two or three years in an eligible facility. The NERLP program may cover up to 85% of your eligible loan balance. You can visit the website at: www.bhpr.hrsa.gov/nursing/loanrepay.htm.

## Law Enforcement or Corrections Officer

This program for law enforcement and corrections officers applies only to Perkins loans. Eligible borrowers may have up to 100% of their qualifying loan balances discharged, and may be eligible for deferment during service time.

As with all Perkins loan programs, you must contact your school for the necessary paperwork. Also keep in mind these loans may qualify for deferment while you are performing the service necessary to qualify your loans for discharge.

## Table 9: Perkins Discharge Options

| Discharge Condition[*] | Amount Forgiven —up to |
|---|---|
| Death | 100% |
| Total and permanent Disability | 100% |
| Teacher- low-income families | 100% |
| Provider-early intervention for disabled | 100% |
| Teacher- math, science, bilingual education, designated teacher shortage | 100% |
| Employee of public or non-profit provider of services to high risk children | 100% |
| Nurse or Medical Technician | 100% |
| Law Enforcement or Corrections Officer | 100% |
| Staff member- education component- Head Start Program | 100% |
| Vista or Peace Corps volunteer | 70% |
| Armed Forces – area of hostilities | 50% |
| School Closure before program of study could be completed | 100%[+] |
| Bankruptcy | 100% |

# Bankruptcy

As mentioned in the Introduction, with rare exceptions, student loans may not be discharged in bankruptcy. Should you attempt to have your loans discharged through bankruptcy, you must be prepared for an adversarial procedure. The courts must determine repayment of your student loans would impose an *undue* hardship on you.

# Additional Programs

In addition to the Stafford and Perkins loan discharge programs, there are state programs available to pay for your education, or to pay you back for your education. Gen and Kelly Tanabe included a chapter on loan forgiveness programs in their book *1001 Ways to Pay for College*. They list state programs alphabetically (by state) and include contact information. Mississippi, for example, has The Critical Needs Teacher Loan/Scholarship (CNTP) program. This program is for junior or senior students at Mississippi colleges or universities. The students must agree to work as full-time teachers in teacher-shortage areas of the state, one year of service for each year of aid received. The award is tuition, fees, a book allowance, and an allowance for room and board.[xxv] If your goal is teaching, you might want to consider whether you can fit this into your educational plan.

---

[xix] http://studentaid.ed.gov/students/publications

[xx] http://studentaid.ed.gov/PORTALSWebApp/students/english/cancelstaff

[xxi] http://studentaid.ed.gov/PORTALSWebApp/students/english/discharges

[xxii] http://studentaid.ed.gov/PORTALSWebApp/students/english/discharges

[xxiii] www.mapping-your-future.org/paying/loanForgiveDetails.htm

[*] Death of borrower or death of student on whose behalf loan was made

[#] Discharge is conditional for three years, must re-certify each year

[+] Borrower must meet requirements

[**] Does not discharge all loans, only applicable loans

[##] Up to $5000 if all conditions are met

[++] Not a discharge-enlistment bonus

[***] Not a discharge, but Educational award may defray part of the loan

[+++] Program may not be funded

[√] Borrower must prove undue hardship in adversarial proceedings

[xxiv] http://studentaid.ed.gov/students/publications

[*] All career discharges are for full-time service

[+] For loans received on or after January 1, 1986

[xxv] Gen and Kelly Tanabe, *1001 Ways to Pay for College*, SuperCollege, LLC, p.305 (2003)

# Chapter 7: Consolidation

*Turning many into one*

Loan consolidation is the process by which the multitude of federal student loans received over the course of education can be brought together into a single loan. (Private loans may be consolidated with other private loans, but not with federally insured loans.)

Consolidation is different from grouped billing. Most lenders will adjust the payment dates of multiple loans to give the borrower a single due date and a single monthly bill. However, unless you, the borrower, take action to consolidate your loans, they remain multiple loans covered by a single Master Promissory Note.

## Advantages of Multiple Loans

Retaining multiple loans is to a student's advantage in many ways. If, for example, your school closes during the course of your education, the loan(s) for that school may be subject to forgiveness or discharge. If the loan disbursements from a closed school were not separate loans, such forgiveness would be more difficult to attain. More importantly, many people obtain their education over an extended period of time. Students may attend school full-time for a year or two, and then drop to half-time. They may stop out of school for a semester, or a few years, and then return full-time. They may change schools more than once, moving from the community college level, to the four-year college/university, and finally to a top-rated graduate school.

Each loan disbursement a student receives may be in a different stage of repayment. Loans which were in repayment when a student left school for an extended period of time may be placed into in-school deferment when the student returns to academia. The older loans will not have a grace period when the student eventually leaves school again, but the new loan(s) will.

The process of consolidation takes all of those old loans and pays them off entirely with the proceeds of a new loan.

Since unconsolidated loans carry a variable interest rate, if rates are high it may be advantageous to stick with the variable rates. In recent years, consolidated loans have been fixed rate, but as previously noted, that changed in June, 2005. Consolidation applications received and processed after June 30, 2005 will be at a variable rate.

At this point in time, if you consolidate your loans, you won't have the fixed rate option.

# Advantages of Consolidation

Consolidation still provides certain benefits to the borrower.

### Interest Rate Calculation

The interest rate on your consolidated loan will not be lower than the interest rates on your multiple student loans[xxvi]. The lender will take a weighted average of the interest rates of all the loans you are consolidating. They will round *up* to the nearest 1/8 of 1%. Obviously, this is a quick and dirty way to estimate your interest rate. Check with your lender for the actual rate you will receive.

It is also important to note that during in-school deferment and your grace period, the interest rate is lower than it will be once you go into repayment.[xxvii] Therefore, if interest rates are relatively low when you graduate, you should consider consolidating immediately after graduation, rather than waiting. Even though you may have missed the fixed-rate window of opportunity, the rate at which you consolidate will determine the highest variable rate for which you may ultimately be responsible.

### Loans Remain Subsidized

One of the advantages of consolidating your student loans is that the loans retain their underlying characteristics after consolidation, and the terms and conditions of your Master Promissory Note remain in effect. If your initial disbursement was prior to July 1, 1993, your consolidated loan will still be governed by the pre-July 1993 rules. The subsidized portion of your loans remains subsidized. The exception to this rule is Perkins loans. If you have subsidized Perkins loans and you consolidate your subsidized Perkins loans and your Stafford loans through a FFEL lender, *your Perkins loans lose their subsidy.* This is one of the major differences between Stafford and Direct loans mentioned in the chapter on types of loans. If you consolidate your subsidized Perkins loans through the Direct loan program, they retain their subsidy[xxviii].

---

**Subsidized Perkins loans do not remain subsidized if you consolidate through a FFEL lender. They do remain subsidized if you consolidate through the Direct loan program.**

---

### Deferment and Forbearance Time Comes Back to You

The deferments for which your loans qualified prior to consolidation remain available to you. In fact, consolidating your loans gives you a brand new loan, and all of the deferment and/or forbearance time you started with when you first obtained your student loans comes back to you. Whether or not the additional deferment and forbearance time is a benefit to you depends upon how well you manage your use of deferments and forbearance on your new loan. If you have abused forbearance in the past and now have no delaying options left to you, this could be an excellent time to consolidate. By doing so, you can start over with a new loan – and this time you can manage it properly.

## Multiple Consolidations

Once you have consolidated, you may not consolidate again. If you think about it, once you have consolidated, you have only one loan – so *how could you* consolidate again? Those wishing to re-consolidate are really asking to do a rate reduction refinance of their loan. At the present time, a rate reduction refinance of student loans is not an available option through the federal loan program. There was much speculation in the news during late spring and summer of 2003 about possibly making a rate reduction refinance option available, but the Department of Education has only a limited amount of money to work with, and they have chosen to make those funds available to students wishing to obtain an education rather than to borrowers who have already completed their studies.

However, if you did not include all of your federal loans when you consolidated, it may be possible to add those forgotten loans. If you go back to school after consolidating, and accrue additional federally guaranteed loans, you may be able to add these new (or forgotten) unconsolidated loans. One individual with whom I spoke recently assured me her lender told her that if she added her new loans to her older consolidated loan, she would be able to retain the fixed-rate option applied to that older loan. Whether or not this is true remains to be seen. The government makes the rules where student loans are concerned, and the lender is not at liberty to vary from those regulations. Keep in mind, consolidation does not lower your interest rate. Your new rate will be a weighted average of the rates on all your loans, rounded up to the nearest $1/8^{th}$ of one percent. Adding additional loans to your consolidated loan will not lengthen your repayment time or add additional deferment or forbearance time.

If you are a credit-worthy individual who consolidated student loans at a higher rate than is now available, you may want to consider a signature loan or a refinance on your home mortgage to pay off the student loans and obtain a lower interest rate.

## PLUS Loans

Parent PLUS loans may be consolidated, but only by the borrower – the parent who took out the loan. This may seem obvious, but many parents take out these loans on the understanding the student will take over the loan after graduation. Taking over the payments is fine, but the loan remains in the parent's name and on the parent's credit, and the loan only qualifies for deferments for which the parent qualifies. In order to take the loan out of the parent's name, the student must execute a new loan which will pay off the old loan(s) in their entirety. The new loan will *not* be a federally insured PLUS loan.

Parents who have taken out loans with the expectation the student will take over the payments after graduation need to be aware of this issue. If there are multiple children, with multiple bundles of PLUS loans, parents may want to consider consolidating each child's loans separately for simplification of payment. Parents must keep in mind, if their student offspring misses making the payments – for whatever reason –the parents must make the payments or suffer the consequences to their credit standing.

Also keep in mind, the death of the borrower discharges the loan. For a student to legally accept the responsibility for an aging or failing parent's debt obligation doesn't make economic sense.


Stafford loans may be consolidated with Direct loans and Perkins loans and SLS loans. All of these types of loans are federally guaranteed, and the subsidized loan portion of the final consolidated loan remains subsidized (with the previously noted exception of Perkins loans consolidated through the FFEL program). The borrower will continue to have available the forbearance and/or deferment for which the original loan(s) qualified. In fact, the borrower could improve his or her options. By consolidating *unsubsidized* Perkins loans with Stafford loans through a lender with liberal forbearance policies (such as SallieMae or Nelnet) the borrower can end up with 5 years of truly discretionary forbearance on the consolidated loan, rather than 3 years (for Perkins loans) of income qualified discretionary forbearance.

## HEAL Loans

HEAL loans may be consolidated with other federally guaranteed loans. However, many FFEL lenders choose to consolidate these loans separately from FFEL loans. HEAL loans are no longer available, so for most of you this is not an issue. For those of you who have not yet repaid or consolidated your HEAL loans, check with the Direct loan program before you take action. Because they are a government entity, they must accept all eligible loans for consolidation. When you make the decision to consolidate, you don't want to be forced to maintain two separate loan accounts simply because of company policy.

# Private Loans

Private loans *may not* be consolidated with federally guaranteed loans. This becomes an issue for students who have excessive student loan debt. The private loans may be subject to consolidation with each other, but they may not be bundled with the federally insured loans.

Let me add one final note about consolidating student loans. If all of your federally insured loans come from a single lender, then you may *only* consolidate with *that lender*. This rule is called, appropriately enough, the *single lender rule*, and this rule has become an issue for many borrowers in the recent wave of consolidations.

After leaving school, most borrowers receive an influx of advertisements offering to consolidate their student loans. If the borrowers don't take advantage of this opportunity immediately, they will certainly receive another round of ads when interest rates decline as they did in July of 2003. However, if all of your loans are with a single lender, the lender may decline to release those loans to another lender for consolidation. Added to this, many lenders will not consolidate low balance loans. Each lender sets its own policies regarding the minimum amount they will consolidate, so you must contact your lender for specific information regarding your loans.

Despite the *single lender rule*, when interest rates hit an all-time low in July 2003, many lenders who by policy would not consolidate low-balance loans also made a policy decision to release those loans (despite the *single lender rule*) to other consolidation sources. Most lenders who *were unwilling* to deal with the expense of consolidating low balance loans *were willing* to allow the borrower to benefit from the low interest rates and lock into a fixed rate loan.

Since lender policies change without warning, you must contact your lender for specific information on consolidating your loans.

---

[xxvi] http://www.financialaid.com
[xxvii] Kelly K. Spors, "Nursing a Debt Hangover From College", *The Wall Street Journal*, WSJ p. 3 ( April 25, 2004)
[xxviii] http:/www.dlssonline.com

# Chapter 8: Payment Options

*It's time to pay the piper*

Federally insured student loans have payment plans[xxix] available to make payments more affordable. The deferment options can delay payment for a period of six months or a year (more in the case of in-school deferment). Forbearance can delay payment for up to one year at a time. However, both of these options may have the drawback of accruing and capitalizing interest. If the payments required to amortize your loan are unmanageable when you enter the repayment mode, those payments are unlikely to become more manageable when they increase over time. You should talk to your lender about your options.

## Standard Repayment Plan

Student loan payments, both Stafford and Perkins, are set to *fully amortize* the loan(s) in a period of ten years. The exception to this rule comes when the fully amortized payment is very, very low. The Department of Education has set the minimum payment requirement at $50 per month for Stafford loans. If you have a loan balance of less than $4,000, you will be required to make this minimum payment, but your loan will be paid off in less than ten years.

## Interest Only

The *'interest only'* option is exactly what it sounds like. You pay the accruing interest on your loans on a monthly basis. By making interest only payments, you avoid capitalization of the interest (as would occur in forbearance, and would occur on unsubsidized portions of your loans in deferment). Most lenders have a two or a four year interest-only option available. Keep in mind, if you pay only the interest, the loan balance never decreases. At the end of your term of interest-only payments, you will be faced with the same payment you were scheduled to make initially. Most lenders also debit your 'forbearance account' for the years in which you opt for interest only payments, which means your 'interest only' option will run out when you run out of forbearance time.

## Graduated Payments

*Graduated payments* plans are 'stepped' payments, which means your payment begins at a lower amount and graduates to higher amounts over time. Your initial payment may be interest-only or even a little less than interest-only. If your payment is less than the interest on your loans, you will be using some of your forbearance time for the graduated payments option. Each year the payments increase. *(Hopefully your income is increasing at the same or a greater rate.)* Your final payment rate will be higher than what you were faced with when the bill first came, because you must now pay the portion of the principal which you did not pay in the early years.

## Income Sensitive

The *income sensitive* program allows you to choose the amount you will pay each month. Your lender will provide you with worksheets and a list of the required documentation. You can then select a payment between 4% and 25% of your gross monthly income. Your payments will adjust annually, based on your gross income from all sources and you will be required to provide proof of income as part of your qualifying documentation each year.

## Income contingent

The *income contingent* program is similar to the income sensitive program in that your payment is based upon income and family size. However, there are major differences as well. The income contingent repayment option is only available through the Direct loan program. This is the second competitive advantage which the government retained for itself. Under this program, your payment varies with your income (as reported on your federal tax returns) and your family size.  However, after making payments for twenty-five years, any remaining balance on the loan will be forgiven[xxx].  Of course, if you've been paying on your loan for twenty-five years (that's not including deferment and forbearance time, when you weren't making payments), you should have the darn thing just about paid off, but if you haven't, you can kiss it goodbye.  The amount forgiven must be declared as income for the year in which it is forgiven, and you must pay taxes on that amount.  For those in the medical and legal professions, where student loan debt can easily top $100,000, this is a definite advantage.  For most people, it will never come into play.  It is, however, one more reason to avoid the trap of the *single lender rule*.  If you have at least one Direct loan, and the future turns out to be less rosy than you had hoped, you can consolidate your loans through the Direct loan program and take advantage of the income contingent payment option.

There are a couple of kickers to the income contingent repayment option.  The first is, the option is not available for PLUS loans.  So PLUS borrowers are likely to be better served by FFEL lenders, simply because private enterprise is easier to deal with *(in my opinion)* than government bureaucracy.  The second kicker is; in order to qualify for the income contingent repayment option, your spouse's SSN is required, and he or she may be required to sign the paperwork.  This *could* have the effect of turning a personal debt into a *community property debt*.  The death of the borrower discharges a student loan.  The death of one borrower, when two parties are responsible on the loan, *may* not result in a discharge.  Read your paperwork carefully.

# Extended Repayment Plan

The extended repayment plan allows you to extend your payments over a longer period of time.  Where the standard repayment plan allows you ten years to pay off your student loans, the extended repayment plan allows up to twenty-five years.  The extended repayment plan is only available to borrowers who have no outstanding FFELP loan balances disbursed prior to October 7, 1998, and who have FFELP loan balances in excess of $30,000.

Since student loans have a total of 60 months of deferment time available (not counting in-school deferments) and up to 60 months of forbearance time (thirty-six months for Perkins loans), you may be paying on your student loans for up to twenty years. If you consolidate half-way through the life of your loan, you can add another ten to twenty years to the term. Even though student loans carry lower than market interest rates (unless you consolidated at the peak of the interest rate climb), this can amount to a great deal of money spent on interest alone.

Back in the sixties and seventies, a large number of people took advantage of the opportunity to go to school on the federal dollar, and after graduation they simply filed bankruptcy. The problem was so wide-spread Congress took action to close that particular loop-hole. As previously mentioned, with rare exceptions, you may not include your student loans in a bankruptcy. You are entitled to file bankruptcy, of course, and you can and should list your student loans as a part of your overall indebtedness. However, your student loans will not be discharged in the bankruptcy, though once your bankruptcy is settled you will have more of your income available to pay on your student loans. But the major purpose of this book is to help you through the student loan repayment process *without* sending you into bankruptcy.

---

[xxix] MPN
[xxx] http:/www.dlssonline.com

# Chapter 9:  Making the Payments

*Some not so real real-world examples*

The best way I know to demonstrate the right and wrong ways to get through your student loans is to use examples.  The following examples are based on fictitious people and imaginary situations.  However, the problems and the solutions are realistic portrayals of what these imaginary people might do in the management of their loans, and what they shoulda (coulda/woulda?) done instead.

## Megan – One way to do it right

Megan is an independent student.  She is the divorced mother of one child.  Megan's parents allowed her to live with them during her college years, providing room and board for her and her baby girl.  They are unable to provide any other financial support.  Megan graduated in 2002 with her teaching credential, having remained in school in the graduate program long enough to obtain the credential which she will need in order to teach.  All of her Stafford loans were disbursed after July of 1993, so she qualifies for the economic hardship deferment.  Unfortunately, some of her loans pre-date 1998, so she does not qualify to have her Stafford loans partially discharged after teaching for five years.  She maxed out on her Stafford loans, with $23,000 in subsidized Stafford loans, and $23,000 in unsubsidized loans.  She also has $18,500 in graduate loans, of which $8,500 are subsidized.  The interest rate on her loans is 5%.

For the purposes of this demonstration I am going to ignore the interest which would accrue on unsubsidized loans while still in school, however I am going to acknowledge the interest which will accrue when Megan leaves school.  Like so many others, Megan does not have employment to go to when she graduates, but she is fortunate enough to begin work after only six months of unemployment following her grace period.  Unfortunately for Megan, her chosen career does not pay extremely well.  At the end of her unemployment deferment (UED),

Megan learned the monthly payments on her student loan debts would be $684.12 per month.

Since Megan's monthly salary was only $2500 per month, this seemed excessive to her. Megan explored the options available to her and decided the economic hardship deferment (EHD) was her best choice. Under that option, if her payments exceeded $500 per month – 20% of gross income – Megan might qualify for deferment. Megan also realized that during deferment, the interest on her unsubsidized loans would accrue and capitalize. So she decided to make the $500 per month payments.

Megan gave written instructions to her lender that everything over the amount required to pay the unsubsidized interest should be applied to principal reduction on her unsubsidized loans. In the absence of written instructions, lenders can and will apply 'overage' as they deem appropriate. After two years of EHD, Megan arranged with her lender to make interest only payments on the full amount of her loan. Once again, Megan chose to pay a little bit more than the interest due each month staying with the $500 per month payment, and she instructed her lender to apply the overage to principal reduction of her unsubsidized loans. Refer to Table 10 for Megan's payment history.

## Table 10: Megan- Doing it Right

| Year | Balance | Total Pmt due* | Total Mo. Pmt. made | Int. pd | Principal Reduction | status |
|------|---------|----------------|---------------------|---------|---------------------|--------|
|  |  | $684.12⁺ |  |  |  |  |
| 1 | $33,000 unsub. $31,500 sub | None | $0 | $0 | $0 | Grace /UED |
| 2 | 34,681.20 31,500.00 | None | 500 | 1,766.85 | 4,233.15 | Additional pmt EHD |
| 3 | 30,448.05 31,500.00 | None | 500 | 1,551.19 | 4,448.81 | Additional pmt EHD |
| 4 | 25,999.24 31,500.00 | 675.69 | 500 | 2,929.32 | 3,070.68 | Forbearance/ Interest only |
| 5 | 22,928.56 31,500.00 | 648.21 | 500 | 2,772.88 | 3,227.12 | Forbearance/ Interest only |
| 6 | 19,701.44 31,500.00 | 626.87 | 500 | 2,608.47 | 3,391.53 | Forbearance/ Interest only |
| 7 | 16,309.91 31,500.00 | 609.87 | 500 | 2,435.69 | 3,564.31 | Forbearance/ Interest only |
|  |  |  |  | 14,064.40 | 21,935.60 |  |

At the end of the seventh year (Megan's sixth year of payment), Megan's lender indicated she could not continue with interest only payments because even though she was paying a little bit extra each month, she would be unable to pay off the loan in the remaining years. The lender suggested Megan consolidate the multiple disbursements into a single loan, and based on the size of her balance, suggested she obtain a twenty year loan. Megan agreed to consolidate.

Over the past six years, Megan paid $36,000 in principal and interest on her loans. Of that, $21,935.60 went to principal reduction, and $14,064.40 went to interest. When she consolidates, she has a balance on her new loan of $42,564.40

Megan decided to go for the ten year payment option, which meant extending the time before she would be debt-free by another six years. By this time, however, she had received enough raises in her income she could increase the monthly payment. Megan wisely decided to raise the amount she chose to pay to $600 per month. Since she now has only a single loan, she does not need to give written instructions to the lender regarding the overage. Megan could easily have set her payments to $550 per month rather than $600, but she chose not to do so. Her goal was to pay a little bit more than was necessary in order to pay off the loan as quickly as possible. Megan paid off her consolidated loan in 7 ¼ years, rather than the scheduled 10 years. Table 11 shows Megan's payment history on her consolidated loan. Since the lender recasts the payments each year in order to fully amortize the loan within the remaining term of the loan, Megan's required payments keep going down as she pays additional principal each month. This means if Megan happens to run into financial difficulties, and is unable to continue making the $600 per month payment, she can drop down to the required payment at any time. The consequence, of course, would be that her loan would not pay off as quickly.

## Table 11: Megan Consolidated

| Year this loan | Year all loans | Balance | Pmt due* | Pmt made | Int. pd | Principal Reduction |
|---|---|---|---|---|---|---|
| 1 | 7 | $42,564.40 | $451.46 | $600 | $2,168.46 | $5,031.54 |
| 2 | 8 | 37,532.86 | 432.28 | 600 | 1,912.12 | 5,287.88 |
| 3 | 9 | 32,244.98 | 408.22 | 600 | 1,642.73 | 5,557.27 |
| 4 | 10 | 26,687.71 | 377.20 | 600 | 1,359.61 | 5,840.39 |
| 5 | 11 | 20,847.32 | 335.74 | 600 | 1,062.07 | 6,137.93 |
| 6 | 12 | 14,709.39 | 277.58 | 600 | 749.37 | 6,450.63 |
| 7 | 13 | 8,258.76 | 155.85 | 600 | 420.75 | 6,779.25 |
| 8 | 14 | 1,479.51 | √ | 600+ | 75.37 | 1,479.51 |
| | | | | | 9.390.48 | 42,564.40 |

## Megan – Doing it Wrong

The story of Megan was designed to show you how student loan debt can be managed without the abuse of forbearance, and without unbearably high payments.  Remember, Megan's scheduled payments would have been nearly $700 per month rather than the $500 payment she chose to make during economic hardship deferment, and then the $600 payment she chose to make after consolidating her loans.  If Megan had simply used the economic hardship deferment, and let the interest on her unsubsidized loans build up, the story would have been very different.

Table 12 shows what typically happens when students who don't understand their options get their first look at the payment statements for their student loans.  You will notice they start out the same, with the grace period and the Unemployment Deferment, during which interest accrues on the unsubsidized loans.  After that, instead of making at least the interest payments on the unsubsidized loans, I simply show the loans in deferment.  After two years of economic hardship deferment, the payments have risen from a little over $684 per month to just over $740 per month.  After that, through the use of forbearance, the borrower is accruing and capitalizing interest on the subsidized loans as well as the unsubsidized loans.  With two years of economic hardship deferment, and five years of forbearance, the loan balance has grown from $64,500 to an overwhelming $89,492.  The student has yet to make a payment, and the payments have risen from $684.13 to $949.21.  Perhaps worst of all, the borrower has run out of the most popular delaying options.

At this point the lender will recommend consolidation as the only reasonable alternative.  By consolidating, the borrower can extend the life of the loan as much as twenty years, putting the payments down around $ 600 per month.

These are both admittedly extreme examples.  There are smart ways to use forbearance and deferment, and not so smart ways.  In the first example, Megan used her deferment and forbearance wisely.  In the second example, she abused both and dug herself into a hole from which she may never emerge.  In the real world, those who follow the first example pay off their student loans, and never have to talk to the bill collectors.  Those who follow the second example spend the rest of their lives hanging up on the collectors and trying to understand where they went wrong.

## Table 12: Megan - Doing it wrong

| Year | Beg. Balance | End Balance | Beg. Pmt[*] | Total | End Pmt[+] | Total | status |
|------|--------------|-------------|-------------|-------|------------|-------|--------|
| 1/2 | $33,000.00 unsub. | $34,681.20 | $350.02 | | $367.85 | | UED |
| | $31,500.00 sub. | $31,500.00 | $334.11 | $684.13 | $334.11 | $701.96 | |
| 1 | 34,681.20 | 36,448.05 | 367.85 | | 386.59 | | EHD |
| | 31,500.00 | 31,500.00 | 334.11 | 701.96 | 334.11 | 720.70 | |
| 2 | 36,448.05 | 38,304.91 | 386.59 | | 406.28 | | EHD |
| | 31,500.00 | 31,500.00 | 334.11 | 720.70 | 334.11 | 740.39 | |
| 3 | 38,304.91 | 40,256.37 | 406.28 | | 426.98 | | forbearance |
| | 31,500.00 | 33,104.78 | 334.11 | 740.39 | 351.13 | 778.11 | |
| 4 | 40,256.37 | 42,307.24 | 426.98 | | 448.73 | | forbearance |
| | 33,104.78 | 34,791.31 | 351.13 | 778.11 | 369.02 | 817.75 | |
| 5 | 42,307.24 | 44,462.60 | 448.73 | | 471.59 | | forbearance |
| | 34,791.31 | 36,563.77 | 369.02 | 817.75 | 387.82 | 859.41 | |
| 6 | 44,462.60 | 46,727.76 | 471.59 | | 495.62 | | forbearance |
| | 36,563.77 | 38,426.52 | 387.82 | 859.41 | 407.57 | 903.19 | |
| 7 | 46,727.76 | 49,108.32 | 495.62 | | 520.87 | | forbearance |
| | 38,426.52 | 40,384.17 | 407.57 | 903.19 | 428.34 | 949.21 | |

# A Farmer's Story Gone Wrong

All his life, John never wanted to be anything but a farmer.  When he graduated from high school, he went off to the local agricultural college and studied farming.  When John finished college, he had a farm and $15,000 in

Stafford loan debt. John's loans were all subsidized, so life should have been pretty easy for him. John had graduated in June, and his payments didn't begin until January of the following year. John had been working part-time on a farm all through college, and was entitled to a share of the proceeds of those crops. Unfortunately, this is the time when things started to go wrong for John.

As a farmer, John did not receive a salary. He had a place to live. He had food on the table. He had a job to do. But he did not have a regular monthly paycheck. In January John received notice his monthly student loan payments would be $ 223.97 per month. (John went to school at a time when interest rates were very high. His payment reflects 13% interest.) John had sold his crops in October, so he had enough in his bank account to simply pay up for the year. He wrote out a check for $2800 and sent it off to his lender with directions to apply it to a full year's payments. Everything was fine that year.

The next year John's crops weren't quite so plentiful. John still received his lump-sum payment when he sold his crops in October, but it was less than he had hoped, and John was courting now. His money had to go further now, and there was less of it. When John received the bill in January, he just couldn't make himself write out the check. He didn't know what emergencies might come up over the next few months. So John started making regular monthly payments instead. Unfortunately, John's lump of money didn't last as long as he had thought it would. There was farm equipment which had to be repaired, and the electric bill went up substantially that year. John made the best decision he could for the good of the farm and stopped making his monthly payments in June. He called his lender to let them know the situation. His lender advised him to use a year of forbearance time.

When John's forbearance expired, in June of the following year, John was down to barely enough money in his account to carry him through until October when the crops would come in. He couldn't risk making even a few monthly payments. There was simply no help for it, so John called his lender and took a second year of forbearance.

John also got married that year, right after the crops came in – in October. The wedding was modest, but still it took a chunk of his ready cash. Mindful of the need to make some progress on his student loans, he sent in a check for $1000, but since his payments were scheduled to be $265.95 per month, he didn't make a great deal of progress on reducing his debt. As you can see,

John's income cycle and his outgo cycle are out of kilter. John will come out of forbearance again in June, at a time when his cash resources are sorely strained. He called his lender, but he didn't know the right questions to ask, so he ended up taking yet another forbearance. And the cycle repeats the next year, and the next. See Table 13.

## Table 13: John - A farmer gone wrong

| Year | Beg Balance | End Balance | Pmt due-mo | Pmt made Yr. | Status |
|------|-------------|-------------|------------|--------------|--------|
| 1 | $15,000.00 | $14,247.14 | $223.97 | $2800.00 | repayment |
| 2 (1st ½) | 14,247.14 | 13,844.43 | 223.97 | 1343.83 | repayment |
| 3 | 13,844.43 | 15,733.86 | 247.86 | | forbearance |
| 4 | 15,733.86 | 16,881.69 | 265.95 | 1,000.00 | forbearance |
| 5 | 16,881.69 | 19,185.63 | 302.24 | | forbearance |
| 6 | 19,185.63 | 21,804.01 | 343.49 | | forbearance |
| 7 | 21,804.01 | 24,779.73 | 390.37 | | forbearance |

By this time, John's loan has grown by nearly $10,000 ($24,779.73 at the end of year 7) and he is no closer to being able to make his payments. John consolidates his loan, because he is now out of forbearance time. Interest rates have gone up during the time when he has not been paying on his loan. Fortunately, at this particular time in the history of student loans, even consolidated loans carried variable interest rates. John feels fortunate he was not locked into a 17% fixed rate loan. However, there is a lower limit on how far the rate can drop, as well as an upper limit on how high it can climb. His rate will never drop below 9%. Since he still can't make his monthly payments, John places his new loan in forbearance for a year. He sends in the payment he believes he can manage in October. He calls his lender to try to arrange for annual payments, but the lender is not prepared to handle annual payments. His lender actually *refuses to accept annual payments*. John continues to use forbearance every year, getting deeper and deeper into debt, with no hope of making progress on the loan.

## What John Could Have Done

John's situation is unique to those who receive their income annually rather than monthly. Annual income presents certain challenges, since most Stafford loan lenders aren't equipped to deal with an annual payment cycle. However, the situation is not hopeless. To begin with, most student loan lenders will allow forbearance in less than 12 month increments. The first thing John needed to do was to get his outgo and his income aligned. He never had a problem making the payments on his farm equipment, because the loan cycle on those loans was set to the crop cycle. When John received his first bill, he paid for a full year, making the payments come due again in January, and it was the off-cycle payment which created his first difficulties. Had the bill come due in October, when his bank account was bulging, he would simply have paid the next annual installment. Then when the combine needed work later in the year, John would have managed some other way. John could have arranged for interest only payments in the year when the crops didn't do so well, or he could have requested forbearance for that single year. Instead, because he didn't know what was available to him, he buried himself in an escalating pile of debt.

The final option available to John at this time is to refinance his student loans with a long-term mortgage on the farm. Because rates have dropped so tremendously in the past few years, if he has enough equity in the farm, he can pay off his high-interest student loan with a low-interest farm loan. This will cause his payments to drop substantially and alleviate the problem of making monthly payments on an annual income. John's local banker understands fully the issues involved in farm lending.

## Judith – Managing a teacher's budget through forbearance

Judith managed to get through college and obtain her teaching credential with a mere $20,000 in Stafford loans. And she was fortunate enough all of her loans were subsidized. Like Megan, when Judith got her first teaching assignment, she discovered $2500 a month doesn't go very far.

Her loans carried an 8% rate, which put her payments at $242.66 per month. She shared an apartment with another teacher at her school, so making the payments – though a strain – did not present an insurmountable obstacle. Unfortunately, although she saved all during the academic year to provide for her needs throughout the summer, when June came around Judith didn't have enough to cover her rent, her car payment, her groceries, and her student loan payments. She let the student loan payment slide. She looked around for part-time work to augment her savings, but didn't find a job she would feel happy doing. July rolled around and she missed her second payment. Within a few days of missing her second payment date, the telephone began to ring. The caller did not leave a message on the answering machine. Judith's roommate answered one morning, and the caller still refused to leave a message. The caller didn't catch Judith until nearly August, when she discovered her lender had turned her file over to the guarantor for collection.

Judith didn't know what to do. She owed $727.98 in payments, plus late fees for the past two months, and she didn't have the money. The representative on the line asked Judith enough questions to know she did not qualify for a deferment, so her options included payment and forbearance. Judith heard the word 'forbearance', and it seemed like a lifeline to her. She quickly agreed to a one year's forbearance, heaved a huge sigh of relief, and promptly forgot all about it. Of course, Judith's forbearance expired in May of the following year. Her loan balance had increased by over $1,600, and her payments – due to begin in June – were now $262.66 per month.

### Let's Rewind Here.

The caller didn't catch Judith until nearly August, when she discovered her lender had turned her file over to the guarantor for collection. Judith didn't know what to do. She owed $727.98, plus late fees for the past two months, and she didn't have the money. The representative asked her when she could go back to making her regular monthly payments. Judith explained that as a teacher, her next paycheck would come at the end of September. The representative then advised Judith she could have a four-month forbearance (June, July, August, and September), with her next payment due in October. He further explained that if Judith could pay the $540 in interest before the end of the forbearance, the lender would not capitalize it, and her payments would not increase. Then he advised Judith she could arrange for another short-term forbearance the following year when school let out for the summer. He told her she didn't need to wait until she was contacted by the lender or guarantor to resolve the delinquency.

After that, Judith made her regular monthly payments October through May, and skipped her payments June through September. It took her a little over thirteen years to pay off her ten year student loan because she used one year of forbearance time every three years.

Most lenders do not require you take your forbearance in one-year increments. Some lenders *will* require a minimum one-year term, so check with your lender for their policy guidelines. Use forbearance as necessary, *but only as necessary*. Forbearance is a lot like *quicksand*. It may look fine on the surface, but if you don't get in and out quickly, it slowly sucks you under. When you've just been given permission to take time off from making payments on your loan at a time when you weren't able to make the payments anyway, it may look like a lifeline, but the cost of forbearance is a higher loan balance, higher payments, and a longer time before you finally get out from under your load of debt.

## When Your Lender Can't Find You

Lamont graduated from college with a degree in Business and a job already lined up. He never stopped out of school, so his grace period was still good. Lamont had grants and scholarships for most of his expenses, but he went to a relatively expensive school, and finished up with the maximum $23,000 in subsidized Stafford loans. He graduated in 2003, when the interest rates were at historical lows. Lamont's current interest rate is 3.88%, and his payments are about $230 per month.

Lamont packed up his belongings and left school for the final time. He drove by his parent's home in Virginia and dropped off all the paperwork he had gathered over the years. He knew he would eventually need to sort through things, but time was short. He needed to get to his new job in Florida and find a place to live. Lamont's new job would be starting in only ten days.

In all the rush of relocating, Lamont forgot to notify his lender of his new address and contact information. January came around, triggering the repayment cycle on Lamont's loans. Lamont was easily in a position to make his payments, but he did not receive the billing information from the lender. Logical, since he forgot to tell the lender about his new address.

When the lender received no response from Lamont, they called his last known telephone number and found it disconnected. The lender mailed to Lamont's last known address, and the mail was returned. As the next step, the lender began to contact Lamont's references.

Lamont's parents refused to divulge their son's whereabouts to an unknown party over the telephone – merely stating he no longer lived or received mail at their address. The lender and the guarantor now have a problem. Neither the lender nor the guarantor's office may divulge to Lamont's parents that their son is delinquent on his student loan payments, and unless the parents know *why* the caller wants to contact Lamont, the parents won't give out Lamont's contact info. The lender leaves messages for Lamont to call, but Lamont doesn't call.

Weeks go by and the parents are becoming more than a little testy over the repeated telephone calls for Lamont, since they have already indicated numerous times that Lamont does not live with them. The telephone calls go on for another three months. Lamont is now six months delinquent on his payments – a very serious situation.

Finally, Lamont happens to be visiting at his parents' house when the lender's telephone call comes in. First thing, Lamont berates the default prevention specialist for harassing his parents. Then he blames the lender for not sending him a bill. Finally, he gives his current contact information, and tells the specialist not to call him at his parents' home again, ever. When Lamont finally cools down – after all, he's really mad at himself for forgetting about his student loans – he considers what he can do to resolve the situation.

Lamont makes a very decent salary. Unfortunately, like so many people, he also spends every dime he makes every month. He bought a new car. The car payments are an outrageous $500 a month, because he had no credit history. He now has several credit cards. Credit card expenses run $400 every month. He bought new furniture for his new apartment. His apartment is new and large and in a fancy complex. Rent is $1500 a month.

Lamont is a single man. He spends about $500 a month on entertainment, and another $800 on groceries and utilities. There really isn't anything left over for student loan payments. Now he has to re-figure his budget to add another $200 plus for student loan payments.

Lamont talks his situation over with the default prevention specialist, who explains there are no deferments for which Lamont qualifies. But the default prevention specialist's job is to cure the account – today, if possible. Forbearance is the only option available. Lamont opts for a year of forbearance, raising his payment about $10 a month, and adding nearly $1000 in capitalized interest.

Had Lamont kept in touch with his lender, he would have known when to expect the loans to come into repayment, and he would have been prepared for them. He might have made the choice of renting a less expensive apartment, or buying a less expensive car, or spending less on furniture and new clothes. Lamont is a responsible person, and he certainly benefited from the education he received, but the student loan bills came due unexpectedly. Now Lamont will work hard to get his credit cards paid down before his student loans come due again. He will consider whether he should move to a less expensive apartment. When he receives his first raise, he will begin sending in monthly payments on his student loans so less of the interest will capitalize.

## PLUS Loans

Herman and Winifred are the aging grandparents of Amber. They have raised Amber since her parents died when she was a teenager. When the time came for Amber to leave high school and go off to college, the thought never occurred to Herman and Winnie not to help her pay her way. When Amber entered college, Herman was still working full-time, and earning a handsome salary. Since PLUS loans are not subsidized, and interest is due from the time of disbursement, Herman has been making the payments regularly.

Amber has long since graduated and moved away, and Herman is planning to retire this year. The loan balance is now $25,000, the interest rate 5%, and there are five years remaining before the loan will be paid off. The payments are $471.78 per month. While he was working, Herman had no problem making the payment, but with retirement, his income will drop substantially.

Herman contacts his lender to find out what he can do to manage his loan better. The lender advises consolidation. By consolidating the loans, Herman can extend the repayment time from the existing five years to fifteen years. Consolidation will drop Herman's payment to $198 a month, which is a manageable amount given his projected income.

Unfortunately, a few years after obtaining the new consolidated loan, Herman develops serious health problems. He is hospitalized for several weeks, and then released to a convalescent facility. Although his income does not change, his expenses increase dramatically. Because of his poor health, Herman does not call his lender, but Winnie does.

Winnie discusses the problems with the customer service representative, and discovers there are no applicable deferments. Winnie requests forbearance paperwork, which she completes and puts in front of Herman for signature. A one-year forbearance will raise the payments to $208, and will capitalize nearly $1,300 in interest. But there is really very little choice. Right now, their funds must be spent on medical expenses. Both Herman and Winnie heave a sigh of relief when they know the PLUS loan has been dealt with for the time being.

During the one year period of forbearance, Herman passes away. There are considerable expenses to be met, but fortunately there is insurance to cover most things. Winnie's widow's pension is about two-thirds of what Herman's income was. Winnie never worked outside the home and has no pension in her own right.

When the PLUS loans come back into repayment, Winnie begins to make the payments as regularly as Herman always did. She never misses a payment, and never questions her need to make the payments. Five more years pass. Winnie develops health problems, though not as serious as those which felled Herman. She spends a few days in the hospital, and a few months in a convalescent facility. During her stay in the care home, Amber makes certain the utilities are paid at the house. A neighbor stops by twice a week to carry in the mail. When Winnie finally returns home, it is to discover the PLUS loan has not been paid for four months. Before she has the opportunity to call her lender and make arrangements, they call her.

When a bill collector calls, they always ask for the borrower by name. They asked for Herman. With a catch in her thin, reedy voice Winnie explains Herman passed away five years ago this month. Winnie then asks if she can have another forbearance, since she has been in the hospital, and really doesn't have the funds to catch up on her missed payments.

The lender, of course, checks the records and discovers the loan was in Herman's name alone. Winnie was never credit-worthy. Winnie is advised to send a copy of Herman's death certificate to the lender, and ignore all future billings.

I won't belabor the likelihood of Winnie receiving a refund for the five years' worth of payments she sent in. The refund will probably happen, but not in a timely manner. Had Winnie known her rights and obligations under the terms of this loan, she need not have scrimped to make those payments after her husband passed away.

## Stay-at-Home Moms

As young people with an eye to the future (or old folks trying to move up in the world) we go to college or trade schools to give ourselves marketable skills so we can support ourselves and our families. However, many find the highest and best use of our educations is in the training and nurturing of children. I have used the term stay-at-home Moms, but the designation will apply equally well to stay-at-home Dads.

Stay-at-home Moms put their careers on hold while they spend their time caring for and teaching the next generation. Sometimes this situation occurs a few years after leaving school, and the student loan is already a part of the monthly budget. But when one of the wage-earners stops earning, the budget usually requires some adjustment.

John and Mary Beth each have student loans on which they have been paying for five years. They now have twin sons, and Mary Beth has left her employment to spend the next few years raising the boys. John still owes $4,000 in subsidized loans, and $6,000 in unsubsidized loans. Current interest rate is 4%. John's payments are $184.17 per month. If he places his loans in forbearance for a year, his payment will increase to $ 191.64 per month. If he uses five years of forbearance – until Mary Beth returns to the active work force, his payments will increase to $224.72 per month.

Mary Beth still owes $12,000, but all of her loans are subsidized. Mary Beth's payments are currently $221 per month. After one year of forbearance, the payments would increase to $ 229.97 per month, and after five years the payments would rise to $269.66. (Of course, when Mary Beth goes back to work, she and John should be able to handle the higher payments, but they will also need to budget for after-school child care if she plans to work full time.)

John and Mary Beth talk the matter over with their lender and discover Mary Beth will qualify to defer her loans under the economic hardship deferment. Student loans are personal loans – not community property loans – and the income qualification for the economic hardship deferment is based upon Mary Beth's *personal income* and not on *family income.* (This is not true for Perkins Loan Economic Hardship deferment. For Perkins loans, the worksheet calls for income from *all* sources. *We can also expect this particular loophole to be closed as soon as it is brought to the attention of the Department of Education.*) Mary Beth completes the paperwork, stating she, personally, has zero income. Her loans are placed in deferment for a period of twelve months.

After taking a serious look at their budget, John and Mary Beth determine they can handle the payments on John's loans and a have little bit extra left over to pay on Mary Beth's loans. Since Mary Beth's loans are all subsidized, there is no interest to pay on her loans. They make the full payment on John's loans and pay $100 per month towards principal reduction on Mary Beth's loans.

After the deferment expires, the payments on John's loans remain the same, $184.17 per month. The remaining balance on Mary Beth's loans has decreased to $10,800, giving her a new payment of $198.90. John and Mary Beth are not yet in a position to make Mary Beth's payments, so they place her loans in deferment for a second year and continue to pay $100 per month towards principal. At the end of the second year, her remaining balance is down to $8,600 and her payment is down to $158.38. John and Mary Beth decide they still are unable to make this payment. They decide to place Mary Beth's loans in forbearance, but continue to make the $100 per month payment to cover the interest as it accrues. Of course, this payment more than covers the interest, so Mary Beth continues to reduce the principal balance.

As you can see from Table 14, after two years of deferment and four years of forbearance (while making a $100 per month payment on Mary Beth's loans), the principal has been reduced enough that the monthly payments will recast to less than $100 per month.

## Table 14: Staying home and getting ahead

| Year | Beg. balance | End balance | Pmts made | New pmt due | Status |
|------|-------------|-------------|-----------|-------------|--------|
| 1 | $12,000.00 | $10,800.00 | $100 | $198.90 | EHD |
| 2 | 10,800.00 | 8,600.00 | 100 | 158.38 | EHD |
| 3 | 8,600.00 | 7,749.19 | 100 | 142.71 | forbearance |
| 4 | 7,749.19 | 6,863.84 | 100 | 126.41 | forbearance |
| 5 | 6,863.84 | 5,942.54 | 100 | 109.44 | forbearance |
| 6 | 5,942.54 | 4,983.83 | 100 | 91.78 | forbearance |

You must keep in mind John and Mary Beth have been making full payments on John's loans this entire time. They have now paid John's loans off entirely (at the end of year five). The twins are five years old, and Mary Beth is ready to return to the work force. She still has five years in which to pay off her student loans, but if she chooses to keep the monthly payment at the $300 per month they have been paying for the past five years, she can be paid off in about eighteen months. She also has one year of forbearance left for emergencies.

As you can see from Table 15 below, if Mary Beth continues with the $300 per month payment in year six (instead of making only the $100 per month payment she and John had been sending on her loans), she can save the additional year of forbearance for emergencies. Of course, before the end of year seven, she'll be paid off entirely, so those emergencies won't have a chance to arise.

## Table 15: Getting further ahead

| Year | Beg. balance | End balance | Pmts made | New pmt due | Status |
|------|-------------|-------------|-----------|-------------|--------|
| 1 | $12,000.00 | $10,800.00 | $100 | $198.90 | EHD |
| 2 | 10,800.00 | 8,600.00 | 100 | 158.38 | EHD |
| 3 | 8,600.00 | 7,749.19 | 100 | 142.71 | forbearance |
| 4 | 7,749.19 | 6,863.84 | 100 | 126.41 | forbearance |
| 5 | 6,863.84 | 5,942.54 | 100 | 109.44 | forbearance |
| 6 | 5,942.54 | 2,544.90 | 300 | 91.78 | Add. pmt |
| 7 | 2,544.90 | 0 | 300 | 57.46 | Add. pmt |

The principles involved remain the same, whether the stay-at-home partner is male or female. The stay-at-home has no income, and therefore qualifies for the economic hardship deferment. In this example, I had John making minimal payments towards Mary Beth's loans. But what if there isn't a partner who can make these minimal payments for you?

## The Wrong Way to Stay at Home

Let's put Amanda in the same sort of situation as Mary Beth, but without a partner to help her out. Amanda is receiving Aid for Dependent Children and Food Stamps while she stays at home to care for her new baby. She has $12,000 in subsidized loans, five years left to pay on them, and no salary.

**Table 16: Staying home and drowning in debt**

| Year | Beg. Balance | End Balance | New pmt. | Status |
|------|-------------|-------------|----------|--------|
| 1 | $12,000.00 | $12,000.00 | $0 | EHD |
| 2 | 12,000.00 | 12,000.00 | 0 | EHD |
| 3 | 12,000.00 | 12,487.25 | 229.97 | forbearance |
| 4 | 12,487.25 | 12,994.28 | 239.31 | forbearance |
| 5 | 12,994.28 | 13,521.90 | 249.03 | forbearance |
| 6 | 13,521.90 | 14,070.94 | 259.14 | forbearance |
| 7 | 14,070.94 | 14,642.28 | 269.66 | forbearance |

When we compare Amanda's situation to Mary Beth's, we see that while Mary Beth was able to pay only $100 per month towards her loan in the first five years, she paid it every month. Unfortunately, Amanda has no salary and therefore makes no payments. During the first five years, when Mary Beth cut her principal to less than half by making $100 per month payments, Amanda added over $1500 to her principal by using three years of forbearance time. Then, during the two years when Mary Beth paid off her loan entirely, Amanda added another $1100 to her balance.

Realistically, there isn't a great deal Amanda can do without an income of any sort. Aid for families with dependent children simply doesn't stretch far enough to accommodate student loan payments. But as you can see, the problem only gets bigger if the loan stays in forbearance. Perhaps Amanda should have considered getting a part-time job so she could have made at least minimal payments. Depending upon her field of study, she might have explored the Full-Time Child Care Provider option for having her loans dismissed. By working as a child care provider, she could have spent the early years with her own child, while at the same time earning enough to support herself, and possibly even qualifying for forgiveness of her loans. Long-term forbearance isn't just *like* quicksand, *it is quicksand*! If you depend upon long-term forbearance to save you, you will ultimately be drowned by your debt.

## New Home Blues

The residential home loan industry is single-handedly responsible for helping thousands of students to drown in forbearance. Before we begin, though, understand there is a world of difference between being *responsible* and being *to blame*.

Derek and Joan are young suburban professionals. They both have good jobs, new cars, and heavy student loan indebtedness. They have managed to save $15,000 for a down-payment on a new house.

Derek and Joan meet with a real estate agent, who shows them their dream house and introduces them to a mortgage broker.

The broker takes a pre-qualifying application. The house requires a $150,000 mortgage. The payment at today's interest rate (6%) will be $900.

Derek and Joan aren't concerned about this payment since the rent on their apartment is $850 per month. They have car loans of $450 and $395, respectively. The property taxes on their new home are expected to be around $150 per month and utilities will be another $300. Derek and Joan have used their credit cards freely for the past several years, so their monthly credit card payments amount to $600 per month. The total sum brings them to $2,795 in monthly expenses. Between them, they bring home $4,200 per month.

Derek owes $30,000 in Stafford loans, only $10,000 of which are subsidized, and Joan owes $25,000, with $5,000 subsidized. Derek's payments on his student loans are $483.15 per month, and Joan's are $402.62. When added to their other indebtedness, their monthly outgo – exclusive of groceries or entertainment expenses – is $ 3,680.77 per month, leaving Derek and Joan about $500 per month for entertainment and to eat on. (Of course, once Derek and Joan are home owners rather than renters, they will have the option of increasing their tax deductions to account for the interest they will be paying, so their take home income may increase slightly.)

After checking all the calculations, the mortgage broker tells Derek and Joan they can qualify for the home loan, but only if they place their student loans into forbearance. Forbearance, the mortgage broker tells them, will free up nearly $900 in monthly cash flow, making the payments easier to handle. The decision is up to them.

Derek and Joan immediately decide to request a year's forbearance on their student loans.

Unfortunately for Derek and Joan, freeing up nearly $900 a month simply meant they spent the extra cash in other ways than making their student loan payments. They bought furniture. They bought appliances. They took a vacation. They ran up their credit cards even further, until the monthly payments exceeded $1,000 per month.

Derek and Joan did not make payments on their student loans, because they did not *have* to. Their loans were in forbearance, after all.

But, after five years of forbearance, they had added over $12,000 to their student loan indebtedness, and just over $200 a month to their *required* payments. And by now their credit cards are so high they can't make the payments anyway. Should Derek and Joan be blamed for not realizing what an attractive web forbearance can create, or how thoroughly stuck they might become? Perhaps not, but they certainly had the information available to them. Like so many others, they never read and understood.

### Table 17: New home forbearance

| Year | | Beg Balance | End Balance | Beg Pmt | End Pmt | Joint Pmt. |
|---|---|---|---|---|---|---|
| 1 | Derek | $30,000.00 | $31,538.36 | $483.15 | $507.76 | |
| 1 | Joan | 25,000.00 | 26,276.63 | 402.62 | 423.14 | $ 930.90 |
| 2 | Derek | 31,538.36 | 33,134.58 | 507.76 | 533.63 | |
| 2 | Joan | 26,276.63 | 27,612.15 | 423.14 | 444.69 | 978.32 |
| 3 | Derek | 33,134.58 | 34,822.63 | 533.63 | 560.82 | |
| 3 | Joan | 27,612.15 | 29,018.86 | 444.69 | 467.35 | 1,028.17 |
| 4 | Derek | 34,822.63 | 36,596.68 | 560.82 | 589.39 | |
| 4 | Joan | 29,018.86 | 30,497.24 | 467.35 | 491.16 | 1,080.55 |
| 5 | Derek | 36,596.68 | 38,461.11 | 589.39 | 619.41 | |
| 5 | Joan | 30,497.24 | 32,050.93 | 491.16 | 516.18 | 1,135.59 |

Their mortgage broker initially advised Derek and Joan to place the loans in forbearance so they could qualify for the home loan. Derek and Joan still had the *right* to make payments on their student loans they simply were not *required* to do so.

Had Derek and Joan continued to make the payments on their student loans instead of spending that 'extra' $900 a month (While they were in forbearance), they could have had their loans almost paid off by the end of the five years they spent in forbearance. Instead, at the end of that time, their only option is to consolidate their loans and start over.

Rather than being nearly free of their student loan debts, Derek and Joan have consolidated their loans, placing their new payment at $465.35 per month for the next twenty years.

## More PLUS Loans

One of the common practices with PLUS loans is to place the loans in the mother's name. Placing the loans in the mother's name is usually done because the father (as the traditional breadwinner) already has a lot of credit. PLUS loans are granted based on credit, with no qualifying ratios or proof of income required, so placing the loans in the mother's name is an easy way for a woman with little or no credit history to establish an independent credit rating.

Placing loans in the mother's name can be a very dangerous practice for women who do not work outside the home. As long as someone else (presumably, in this instance, the husband) is making the payments on the loans, there are no problems to be resolved. If the husband should die, or if the parents separate and the husband no longer makes the payments on the student loans, the financial consequences to the woman can be disastrous.

PLUS loans are not subsidized loans. Deferment and forbearance have the same consequences in that all interest accrues and is capitalized. Interest accrues from the date of disbursement. This means while the student is in school, the parent must either make payments or place the loan in forbearance and expect to pay more at the end of the forbearance.

In order to qualify for deferment, the *borrower* must qualify for the deferment. If the parent borrower is in school, the loan will qualify for an in-school deferment, but the interest will still accrue. If the parent borrower is unemployed, or has zero income, the loan will qualify for an unemployment or economic hardship deferment, but the interest will still accrue. These are important distinctions which many borrowers do not fully comprehend.

## Underage Students

Danita was a very bright teenager who graduated from high school at seventeen and went right on to college. Because she was only seventeen when she entered college, she could not take out a Stafford loan in her own name. Danita's mother took out the loan on Danita's behalf – a PLUS loan. When Danita's mother took the loan, the financial aid office helped her to place the loan in forbearance for the first year.

With the coming of the second semester, Danita had already reached her eighteenth birthday and was able to arrange for a subsidized Stafford loan on her own.

The following September, the forbearance on the PLUS loan expired, and Danita's mother had the option of placing it back into forbearance or beginning repayment.

Danita's Mom had taken out a $5,000 loan for her daughter's first semester, but somehow she had not understood the loan would be in repayment immediately. She believed the loan would be in in-school deferment and would transfer to Danita's name as soon as Danita reached her eighteenth birthday. It doesn't happen that way. Since the loan was small, and the interest rate low, Danita's Mom had the choice of making $53 per month payments now, or placing the loan back into forbearance and making $55 per month payments next year. Wisely, she decided to begin paying on the loan immediately.

Kimberly's Mom was faced with a different situation. Kimberly was a very indifferent student in high school, excelling only in her drafting classes. Kimberly was recruited by one of the local trade schools for their CAD drawing program. They explained to Kimberly and her parents that she could complete their program in only a few short months instead of spending four or more years in a college program.

Kimberly's parents talked it over with Kimberly, and the family decided the CAD drawing program was the best option for her. Kimberly entered the training program as soon as she left high school in June.

Kimberly too, was only seventeen at the time she entered post-secondary school. Kimberly's Mom signed for the PLUS loan. Kimberly soon discovered that although the program was designed to speed her through the training in a very short time, she was, *heaven forbid*, required to study. And she was *also* required to study things she had no interest in studying, like geometry and trigonometry, and calculus. Kimberly was promptly dropped from the program after only six weeks because she would not keep up with her class work.

Kimberly's Mom was less than pleased. Unfortunately, she now had a $10,000 unsubsidized loan to pay back, for an education her daughter did not receive. She saw no reason she should pay the loan, and wanted to sue the school.

Kimberly's Mom may or may not have a cause of action against the school. Only her attorney can advise her on such a matter. However, the school and the lender are two separate entities. The lender loaned her money in good faith, and Kimberly's Mom is obligated to repay the loan.

## Officer Bruce

Bruce graduated with a degree in Criminal Justice and a desire to be a police officer. He completed his training with the local police department, and began working as a rookie, making a princely salary of $35,000 per year. Bruce has $20,000 in Perkins loans. His payments are $212.13 per month. Bruce is a divorced man, with two small boys to support. Two hundred dollars a month is a strain on his budget. Bruce contacts his school and determines forbearance is available to him. They also tell him about the deferment option, and the possibility his loans may be discharged for his service as a police officer. They explain to him that if he uses forbearance, his loan balance will increase by over $1,000, and his payments will go up to $222.94 per month. The school sends Bruce the necessary paperwork, and he places his loans in deferment while he performs his public service as a police officer. Eventually all of Bruce's loans are discharged as a result of his work in public service. Had Bruce's loans been Stafford loans, the story would have been different. Stafford loans do not qualify for discharge for police department service, nor do they qualify for deferment.

# Nurse Andrew

Andrew graduated and passed his state boards as a registered nurse. Andrew has $15,000 in Perkins loans (5% interest rate) and $25,000 in Stafford loans (4% interest rate). Andrew is the type of person who always checks out his options before making major career decisions.

The first thing Andrew did after graduation was contact NERLP about the possibility of working in an eligible facility. He was fortunate enough to be hired, and signed a three-year contract.

Andrew's payments on his Perkins loans were scheduled to be $159.10 per month. However, since he was working in the nursing profession, he was able to defer his payments on his Perkins loans, and after three years NERLP paid $12,750 towards his qualifying loans, leaving him a Perkins loan balance of $2,250.

Andrew also had the Stafford loans, half of which were subsidized. However, there is no qualifying deferment for Stafford loans. His Stafford loan payments were $253.11 per month. Andrew set up an automatic draft from his checking account to make this monthly payment, insuring it was made on time every month. Table 18 shows Andrew's payment history, and the benefits of automatic payments.

You will notice at the end of years four and eight, Andrew applies the on-time payment rebate he has earned to principal reduction. Applying the payment rebate to principal reduction allows Andrew to pay off his Stafford loans in nine years and five months, rather than the ten years he was expecting.

After Andrew's three year contract, NERLP has paid off 85% of his Perkins loans. His payment to amortize the remaining balance over ten years would be $23.86 per month, but Andrew instead chooses to make a minimum payment on his Perkins loans of $50 per month. His Perkins loans are paid in full during years four through eight, with only three payments due in year eight. Should Andrew choose to divert that $50 per month towards his Stafford loans, he can pay them off a year earlier as well.

**Table 18: Combining discharge and deferment with repayment**

| Year | Perkins balance | End balance | Stafford balance | End balance | Annual Pmt | Status |
|------|-----------------|-------------|------------------|-------------|------------|--------|
| 1 | $15,000.00 | $15,000.00 | | | $ 0 | deferment |
| | | | $25,000.00 | $22,977.78 | 3,037.32 | repayment |
| 2 | 15,000.00 | 15,000.00 | | | 0 | deferment |
| | | | 22,977.78 | 20,814.32 | 3,037.32[*] | repayment |
| 3 | 15,000.00 | 15,000.00 | | | 12,750.00[v] | deferment |
| | | | 20,814.32 | 18,568.58 | 3,037.32 | repayment |
| 4 | 2,250.00 | 1,764.63 | | | 600.00 | repayment |
| | | | 18,568.58 | 15,386.99 | 3,887.77[+] | repayment |
| 5 | 1,764.63 | 1,254.53 | | | 600.00 | repayment |
| | | | 15,386.99 | 12,934.85 | 3,037.32 | repayment |
| 6 | 1,254.53 | 718.44 | | | 600.00 | repayment |
| | | | 12,934.85 | 10,389.45 | 3,037.32 | repayment |
| 7 | 718.44 | 155.04 | | | 600.00 | repayment |
| | | | 10,389.45 | 7,747.25 | 3,037.32 | repayment |
| 8 | 155.04 | 0 | | | 155.04 | |
| | | | 7,747.25 | 4,161.11 | 3,887.77[#] | repayment |
| 9 | 0 | 0 | 4,161.11 | 1,282.04 | 3,037.32 | repayment |
| 10 | 0 | 0 | 1,282.04 | 0 | 1,282.04 | |

Over the course of just under ten years, Andrew has managed to pay off – or have paid for him – $40,000 in student loan debt. His payments never rose above $303.11 per month for all loans, and through the use of automatic checking account deductions, Andrew has managed to have his lender not only reduce his interest rate, but also pay $1700 towards his principal.

## No New Home Blues

You need to be aware you may have received more than one disbursement in a given time period. Charles found himself in an unfortunate situation because he did not realize he actually received two disbursements at a time. Charles attended a trade school, training to be a slot machine technician. Charles received two disbursements his first term, one subsidized and one unsubsidized, for a total of $5,000. Because he received both disbursements at the same time, he didn't pay attention to the details of his loans and thought of them as a single loan. Then Charles stopped out of school the next term. His two loans went into their grace period. When he returned to his training after a few months off, the school arranged for his existing loans to be placed back into in-school deferment while he completed his education. When he finished the second term, those first two loans went into repayment immediately, while the second two loans (another $5,000) went into their grace period. Unfortunately, Charles didn't read the paperwork which came to his last known address. Charles relied on his understanding of the grace period, rather than double-checking, and he 'knew' he wasn't in repayment yet. So he ignored the notices.

Employment opportunities were slim for his chosen profession in rural West Virginia. Charles did not find a position right away, and he continued to ignore the notices which came in the mail. He avoided answering the telephone. He moved and gave no forwarding address. Eventually the guarantor on his loan made contact with him and explained he was in default on his two loans. Now remember, Charles attended school for two terms, and he believes he has two loans. In fact, he has four loans. Two of his loans are subsidized, and two are unsubsidized, and the two sets of loans came into repayment six months apart. The first two came into repayment as soon as he finished school, and the second two still had their grace period to run. So when Charles made arrangements with the guarantor to rehabilitate his two loans, he thought he was taking care of the entire situation.

At this point his second two loans were delinquent, but not yet in default. The guarantor's office continued collection efforts on the two loans not in default, but every time Charles talked to someone from the guarantor's office, he explained he was already handling the situation with another department. Naturally, the two departments never checked with one another. So now Charles is diligently making payments on his first two loans, believing he only has two loans, and his second two loans are being ignored – and eventually going into default.

After six months of making payments on the defaulted loans, Charles attempts to purchase a home. The credit report comes back showing the defaults. Charles knew he had credit issues, and he never believed he would be able to qualify for an "A" loan, but he also knew there are mortgage companies who specialize in less than perfect borrowers. He had carefully selected one of these "B" to "C" brokers. After reviewing the credit report, the broker told Charles his attempts to rehabilitate his credit had not yet gone far enough. He explained to Charles the six months of rehabilitation on the first two loans would normally enable him to qualify for a home loan – though not at a desirable interest rate. However, the two defaulted loans – the ones not in rehab – would prevent him from obtaining a home loan until he had followed the same procedure with them.

Charles made a number of mistakes. First, he didn't read his paperwork, so he didn't know what loans he had and what rights he had. Charles might have qualified for deferment (unemployment or economic hardship). He definitely qualified for forbearance. Second, he failed to keep in touch with his lender. One simple conversation with the lender would have put him on notice there were in fact four loans to be dealt with rather than two. Third, he ignored the telephone calls and letters sent to him by both his lender and the guarantor. He actively refused all the offers of help which came his way.

Charles' mistakes won't keep him from getting a home loan permanently, but they will definitely delay his dreams. Once he has made regular payments on the second two loans for a period of six months, his mortgage broker may be able to find him a loan. The interest rate will be higher than he might have hoped for, and there may be higher up-front fees involved, but Charles will eventually be able to buy a home. Of course, it won't be the house he had picked out. Adding these two additional loans into his debt ratios may cause him to qualify for a smaller loan, and four defaults instead of two may cause the lenders to take a harder look at his credit. And his dream house will have been long since bought by someone else.

## D'Artagnan and the "I'm in jail" deferment

D'Artagnan graduated from college with an MBA and went to work immediately as a stock broker. He drew an excellent salary and had no problems making his monthly payments. For the first few years of his career, he was bringing money home by the wheel barrowful. Like most young people, he and his wife also spent almost as fast as the money came in, but D'Artagnan knew the power of compounding, and he made sure a goodly percentage went into savings.

Unfortunately, D'Artagnan enjoyed the challenge of the stock market a little too much. He was scooped up in one of the 'insider trading' scandals, and had to spend three years in jail. During his period of incarceration, his wife continued to make the payments on his student loans, on their joint credit cards, and on their home and cars. The market crashed, and their savings evaporated at a frightening rate. His wife sold his car and the house and moved into a small apartment with their three children. But the house was heavily mortgaged and the housing market was slow, they owed more on the cars than they were worth and she didn't realize enough from the sales to be much help. Six months before D'Artagnan was scheduled to be released form jail, his wife stopped making payments on his student loans and shortly thereafter she applied for welfare for herself and their two children. When the lender started calling, she didn't want to discuss her husband's incarceration, so she simply told them he was unavailable. When the guarantor started calling, she did the same thing. She tossed the letters and delinquency notices in the garbage since she didn't have the money to pay the bill.

By the time D'Artagnan rejoined his family, his loans were well on their way to default. He had no money, no job, and no prospects. Fortunately, he was home when the next call came in from the guarantor's office. Once D'Artagnan got past his anger that the guarantor and the lender had been, in his words, 'harassing' his wife, he was ready to listen. After only a few moments, he realized there was a way to salvage the situation. D'Artagnan had been in jail for the past three years, including the period of his delinquency. His income during that time period had been considerably less than Federal Minimum Wage. At the time he was contacted, he was receiving public assistance in the form of Aid for Needy Families and Food Stamps. His federal education loan debt most definitely exceeded 20% of his gross monthly income. Once the proper paperwork for an economic hardship deferment had been completed and processed, D'Artagnan was no longer delinquent on his loans.

# Unemployment Happens

Despite our best efforts, many of us will end up unemployed at some point in our lives.  We may be in that situation because we left a perfectly good job to stay home and take care of children, but now we are trying to return to the work force.  We may leave a job because we wish to relocate – for whatever reason – to another part of the country.  The company we work for may down-size.  Our positions may be shipped overseas.  We may not have liked what we were doing and wanted to change careers.  Or we may not have been any good at what we were doing and were fired.  Now we are trying to reenter the work force.

The actual reasons for your unemployment are not relevant to the Unemployment Deferment.  In order to qualify for the Unemployment Deferment, you must be substantially unemployed and actively seeking permanent, full-time work in any field.  If you are working twenty hours a week because you cannot get work forty hours a week, and you are looking for full-time work, you probably qualify.  If you have been a stay-at-home parent for the past few years, but are now actively seeking full-time employment outside the home, you probably qualify.

However, if you were unhappy in your last position and quit so you could open your own business, and you are working like a demon trying to get your new business off the ground, you probably *do not* qualify since you are not actively seeking full-time employment.  *(You might want to look into the possibility of qualifying for the economic hardship deferment instead.)*

## Your Best Option is Deferment

If your loans are subsidized, and you qualify for the Unemployment Deferment, your best option is to place your loans in deferment.  Then if you have the resources to make payments, do so.  Making payments has no effect on qualification and *will not* throw you out of deferment or forbearance.

Having the loans in deferment protects your credit if you are unable to make the payments.  Allowing the government to make your interest payments for you will be financially beneficial to you while you can't make your payments.  Remember, for subsidized loans, the balances don't go up during deferment the way they do during forbearance.

---

* The lender will re-cast payments yearly in order that the payments may fully amortize the loan over the expected re-payment period of 10 years. Payments shown are what would be required to pay off the loan in this time period.

+ This is the standard payment required to fully amortize the loan within 10 years. During grace, deferment, and forbearance no payments are actually due.

* Again, the lender will re-cast the payment based on the outstanding balance so that the loan will be fully paid off at the end of the term.

√ No payment is shown here. Amortizing the remaining balance over the remaining term of the loan yields a payment in the range of $50, but the loan will be paid off in only three payments.
+ Two equal payments of $600 and a final payment of $354.88

* During forbearance and deferment, no payments are required. Payments are shown here to demonstrate what they would be if the loan were in repayment rather than deferment or forbearance.
+ The payment rises each year because the balance rises with the capitalized interest.
* After 12 months of on-time payments through automatic checking account deductions, the lender drops the interest rate by ¼% so more of the payment applies to principal reduction.

√ This is the payment from NERLP. Andrew has made no payments so far on these loans.

+ After 48 on-time payments through automatic checking account deductions, Andrew's lender gives him a 7% rebate on his payments – which he applies to principal reduction.

# Another 48 on-time payments have been made.

# Chapter 10:  Loan Management

This chapter is not a list of tricks to avoid paying your student loan.  There are no *tricks* for debt management.  There are, however, techniques.

## The Dos and Don'ts of Student Loans

**Choose Your Loans Wisely**

By this time you realize there are differences between Perkins loans and Stafford/Direct/Ford loans.  The differences include the amounts you may borrow, the interest rate, the deferments available, and the discharges available.

If you are planning a career in public service, you need to make sure as much of your student loan debt as possible is from the Perkins program.  Go back and read the Chapter on discharges and loan forgiveness one more time.  With Stafford loans (and only with recent Stafford loans) a teacher can have up to $5,000 of student loan debt forgiven.  With Perkins loans (retroactively) a teacher can have up to 100% of his or her student loan debt forgiven.  Need I say more?

On the other hand, if your career goal is to work on Wall Street, the Stafford/Direct loans are currently carrying a lower interest rate.  You business types will certainly understand the significance of lower interest.

**Auto-Debit**

Many, but not all lenders will allow you to arrange for your payment to be automatically debited from your checking or savings account[xxxi].  Those lenders who do allow auto-debit frequently reward their borrowers for participating in this program.  Some rewards you may earn include;
- A lower interest rate on your loan after you have made a certain number of on-time payments.  This may also be a stepped interest rate reduction,

with one step after twelve on-time payments, and a second after another twelve or twenty-four.

- A rebate after a designated number of on-time payments. This rebate may be in the form of a check or a credit against the principal balance of your loans.

Since the above programs are lender-specific and subject to change, you need to check with your lender to be certain you take advantage of every benefit offered to you.

Auto-debit, in addition to earning you financial rewards, insures you do not forget to make your payments in a timely fashion, and saves you the hassle of writing the check once a month, finding a stamp, running down to the post office (we all know we aren't supposed to put our bills – checks enclosed – out where they may be picked up by strangers). Automatic-debit will also come in handy for you when you decide to take an extended vacation. The bank will continue making your payment, and you won't need to find someone you trust to mail your checks for you.

It is important to know you cannot set up an automatic deduction from your checking or savings account while you are in forbearance or deferment. Since payments are *not required* while the loan is deferred, the lender is unable to accommodate you with automatic deductions. While in deferment or forbearance, you certainly may make payments – either on-line or by mailing a check – but your payments cannot be automated by the lender.

About thirty days before your forbearance or deferment ends, you should receive a new coupon book from your lender (if your lender uses coupon books) and there should be an auto-debit form included in the coupon book. Fill out the form and mail it in along with a voided check to set up an automatic payment. You can also go on-line to your lender's website and download the form, or call your lender and request that they send you a form.

## Make a Budget

A budget doesn't have to be complicated. List your monthly expenses in one column and your monthly income in another. You'll know right away if you have a problem. If you spend ten percent less than you earn, you will be relatively rich. If you spend ten percent more than you earn, you will most likely end up in bankruptcy. And if you invest the ten percent which you don't spend, the magic of compounding will work for you and you will retire wealthy – or take a wonderful trip to Tahiti.

## Look for an Employer Who Will Pay Your Student Loans

This isn't an impossible goal. Many employers will offer this as a signing incentive to newly graduated hires. They may require you to work for them for a full year before they disburse the funds, but it's worthwhile to investigate the possibilities. Many of them also have programs to help fund your further education. When you interview, explore these options.

## Check Alternate Loan Repayment Programs

Both *Financial Aid 101* and *1001 Ways to Pay for College* have lists of aid available through various state programs. Check to find out if you qualify for one of these special deals.

Check out UPromise[xxxii] on the internet. This is a program which credits a percentage of your qualifying purchases towards your college expenses. When you're saving for college, this can be a tremendous help. A friend of mine used the program to consolidate her existing loans through UPromise, and tells me her purchases are going towards repaying her consolidated loan. She also tells me the program is new enough there are still 'bugs' to be worked out, so be patient. There is no cost to join – for you or the friends and family you invite to save on your behalf – so it certainly can't hurt you.

## Make a More than Minimum Payment

The minimum payment is designed to allow you to pay off the loan in full in a ten year period. If your loan balance is very low, or if the interest rate is very low, your minimum payment may be $50 and may pay off the loan in less than ten years. If your budget is so tight the minimum is all you can manage, it will take you the full ten years to pay off this debt. If you can manage as little as $10 extra each month, you will pay off your loan faster. Always designate – in writing – where you want the extra money applied. If you have no unsubsidized loans, simply start with the oldest or the smallest loans and work your way through them. If you have unsubsidized loans, always have the extra applied to the principal of one of your unsubsidized loans. Remember, in the absence of written instructions, your lender will apply any extra payment as they deem fit – usually across the board with a percentage going to each loan.

## Avoid Credit Card Debt

Credit cards generally carry a higher rate of interest than your student loans, your home mortgage, and your car loan *(probably combined!)*. In many cases, they will charge as much as 25% annual interest. Credit card companies rarely allow you to skip payments when you hit a rough patch financially. If they do allow you to skip one or even two payments, they will continue to charge you interest (forbearance). They may be willing to sell you an insurance product which will make minimum payments for you when you are out of work, but you will pay for the insurance, and the payment the insurance company makes will be minimal. Credit cards are a wonderful invention for getting us through emergencies, but keep them for *true* emergencies. Unless you are the type of person who charges everything and *pays the card off every month*, leave the card at home and rely on current income for current needs. Employing discipline in the use of credit cards will help you avoid overspending your monthly budget.

## Buy a Less Expensive House

If you cannot qualify for a home mortgage without placing your loans in forbearance, find a less expensive house. Wait until you have saved a larger down payment. Wait for interest rates to go down. The national economy has had some serious ups and downs in recent years, and most of us can no longer depend upon regular raises every year. If you put your loans in forbearance hoping next year your income will go up significantly, you may be burying yourself in a mortgage *and* drowning in forbearance.

## Choose Deferment over Forbearance, and Make Interest Payments

If you qualify for a deferment, *and* you cannot make your payments, use the deferment, even if your loans are not subsidized. Of course, if your loans are subsidized, deferment will make a significant financial difference for you. But even if your loans are not subsidized save forbearance time for a real emergency. If you choose forbearance when you could have used deferment, and a time comes when you need the time off but do not qualify for deferment, you will regret your choice.

## Keep Making Payments, even in Deferment or Forbearance

If you must use deferment or forbearance, try to make some kind of minimal payments. You do not want the interest to accrue and capitalize any more than is necessary. You certainly do not want to be in worse shape after your time off than you were in before you took a break from payments.

## Consolidate When Interest Rates are Low

The Department of Education determines the interest rate (for Stafford and PLUS loans) in May for the year beginning in July. Many, but not all, lenders will 'hold' a consolidation package for the best rate, but until the rate is announced, your lender does not know exactly what the next year's rate will be. Lenders do have an idea what interest rate range is coming and can advise you of what to expect. If you have not consolidated your loans, check with your lender in April or May. They will be able to tell you whether they expect the new rate to be higher or lower than the current rate.

Consolidation may lower your payments as much as 50%, so if you are having difficulty making the standard payment, consolidation may be your best option. Remember, a consolidated loan may be paid back over a longer time period. A longer time period in which to repay results in lower payments (but more interest paid). Also remember, the government has set the minimum payment at $50 per month for newer loans. If consolidation does not lower your payments, you still may choose to go forward with consolidation because you may be able to start over again with deferment and forbearance – and do it right.

Keep in mind, the interest rate on your loans is lowest when your loans are in in-school deferment or the succeeding grace period. The interest rate for your consolidated loan is based on the interest rates of all your existing loans.

## Use Forbearance Stingily

Each lender sets its own forbearance policy and you may be allowed anywhere from twenty-four to sixty months of forbearance time. During forbearance, your loans will grow by leaps and bounds unless you pay the interest. Get in the habit of making your payments, and when you absolutely must take time off, continue to make payments – just make smaller payments. Because each lender sets its own policy regarding forbearance (with the exception of mandatory forbearance) not all of them will allow you to take only a few months at a time. Many lenders will only allow forbearance only in six or twelve month increments. For the teacher trying to manage summers without income, a long forbearance time can make things difficult. If your lender allows smaller increments of forbearance time, use the shortest amount of time necessary to get you by. Interest may be capitalized as frequently as quarterly, and is always capitalized at the end of the forbearance. If you are not able to make interest payments, you will want to have the smallest possible amount of interest capitalized.

## When you Can't Make a Payment, Call your Lender

Discuss your options with them. They can't help you if they can't talk to you and find out what the problem is. If you do need to take a few months off in forbearance, your lender may be able to handle the matter over the telephone, with no paperwork to complete. If you call your lender, they may never have to report a delinquency to the credit bureaus, which will protect your credit.

## Don't Depend on Credit Counseling Companies to Solve your Student Loan Problems

Credit counseling companies provide a tremendous service to a lot of people in this country, but they do not have great success in helping with student loans.

Credit counseling companies have their hands tied simply because the student loan is federally guaranteed or federally funded. The lender on a student loan is unlikely to accept a smaller principal amount when they know they can recover the full principal amount from the government if you default. You are already paying a lower than market interest rate, so the credit counseling company likely will not be able to negotiate a lower rate for you. The government has determined the minimum payment is $50 per month, so the credit counseling company is not likely to be able to negotiate a lower payment for you. If you are paying more than $50 per month, your lender will likely lower your payment for you without the need to have a third party involved. If you find yourself in need of the services of one of these companies, by all means work with them. But do not expect them to be able to alleviate your student loans. Let the credit counselor know what your monthly payments on your student loans are, and then make the payment yourself. Since they won't be able to negotiate a lower payment, a lower amount, or a lower interest rate, you might as well maintain control.

## Keep Track of the Dates when Deferment or Forbearance Ends

Should you place your loans in deferment or forbearance, mark on the calendar the date when the next payment is due. Forbearance and deferment are both applied retroactively to the time when the qualifying condition began – the date you became unemployed, for example – or the date when the delinquency began if you are delinquent at the time you take action. Deferments last for a period of six or twelve months, but if applied retroactively, you may be back into repayment next month instead of six months from now. As you may recall from previous reading, your lender may count time differently from you and I, so having missed one payment, you may be 58 days delinquent. Your lender will tell you when your post-forbearance or post-deferment payment is due. They will also send you a notice approximately thirty days before the forbearance or deferment ends. If you write your next due date on the calendar, you won't need to hunt high and low for the notice.

## Keep in Touch With your Lender

Each lender has different policies, and no book can cover all of the policies of all of the student loan lenders in the country. Your best source for information about your lender's policies is your lender. Your lender wants you to successfully pay off your student loans in the shortest time possible. It is not in their best interests for you to use excessive forbearance, despite the accruing interest, and it is certainly not in their best interests for you to default on the loan. But, they cannot help you if you do not keep in touch with them. If you move, call and give your lender your new address. Make sure they always have a current telephone number for you. If you marry or change your name, notify your lender of the change. If you are unemployed, terminally ill, receiving welfare, the new mother of quintuplets – let your lender know. Lenders are experts on working the system of deferments and forbearances and arranging flexible payment plans. Give your lender the opportunity to help you.

## Double-check Partial Discharge/Loan Repayment Options

Programs change, so at least once a year, visit the Department of Education website to verify program availability and qualifications. You may be in for a pleasant surprise! Do the same with your state Department of Education website. Many states have special programs for their residents – particularly for those in the teaching and health care professions. As a tax-payer, you are helping to fund these programs. You may just as well take advantage of the ones which apply to you.

## Go Back to School

There is no time limit on the amount of in-school deferment you can have, so long as you are enrolled at least half time. Of course, your unsubsidized loans will accrue interest while you are in school, unless you make interest payments. However, advanced training may allow you to move up in your career, generating greater income potential. Most state colleges and community colleges are still very affordable. If your loans are not current, you may not be able to receive financial aid, so make certain everything is current and go learn something new. If you incur additional student loan debt, you may be able to consolidate your old loan(s) and your new loans at a better interest rate, and of course consolidation stretches out the time you have to pay the loan back. Keep the *single lender rule* in mind if you seek additional loans, since you may want to be in a position to choose a different lender for your consolidation.

## Choose Your Lender Wisely

If you already have your student loans, it's too late to interview lenders. On the other hand, if you're just starting to explore the loan options available to you, find out exactly what each lender has to offer. A lender who offers five years of forbearance – with no qualifying restrictions – may be easier to work with in the long run than one who offers only two years of forbearance. You don't want to use the extra time, but having it as a safety net may be comforting. A lender who allows you to take three months of forbearance instead of twelve months at a time may make your loans easier to manage. Make certain you have at least one loan through the Direct loan program, especially if you also have Perkins loans. Make sure your Direct loan is the last one you obtain, since you may not be allowed to return to FFEL lenders once you have entered the Direct loan system. You may want to consolidate through Direct loans to take advantage of their income contingent repayment option, if life hands you lemons. If all of your loans are Stafford loans, even though you personally select six different FFEL lenders, they may all sell your loans to a single lender and you may find yourself trapped by the *single lender rule*.

## Don't Have a Mortgage Burning Party

Many of us old-timers will remember the episode from "MASH" when Colonel Potter and his bride finally made the last payment on their home mortgage. With great ceremony, the good Colonel burned the mortgage document. *Do not follow suit.* When you make your final payment on your student loan, and you receive a letter from your lender indicating your loan is fully paid, file the letter carefully away and keep it forever. If you want to have a little ceremony, burn a copy. *Keep the original.* Someday, a default prevention specialist may call you up and explain you are now ninety days delinquent, and when can you send the money? You can send them a copy of the letter. Mistakes happen – even in lender's offices. Life will be much easier for you if you can simply supply the proof you no longer owe anything.

## Consult a Good Tax Accountant

Interest on student loans may be tax deductible (depending on your other itemized deductions). The principal you pay on your student loans may be a tax credit. Don't ignore these potential benefits. In addition, the Department of the Treasury has recently (May 6, 2004)[xxxiii] determined the origination fee you paid in order to obtain your loan is tax deductible. This fee must be spread out over the term of the loan (ten years in the case of a standard repayment plan). They have also determined the capitalized interest (during deferment for unsubsidized loans and during forbearance for all loans) may also be tax deductible. Since most lenders do not report these items separately each year, you will need to do a little research in order to determine the amount of deduction you may have available to you. Consult with a qualified tax accountant to see if you can get more out of your student loan debt by deducting the interest you paid, the origination fee you financed, the capitalized interest you are now paying interest on, or by applying the amount you paid towards principal as a credit towards your annual federal income taxes. *Remember, you may be able to file an amended return for past years as well.* Don't let these tax deductions and credits go to waste.

## If You Become Unemployed, Notify your Lender

Do not wait until your payment is due hoping you will have found a new job by then. Go on-line and download the necessary forms, or call your lender and request they be mailed or faxed to you at once. Complete the forms as soon as you receive them, and return them to your lender in the manner they require. (Some lenders will not accept faxes. Many do not allow electronic filing. Everyone accepts U.S. Mail.) Follow-up with your lender about a week after you send the forms. If you have a new job by then, you can tell the lender to ignore the request because you are once again employed. Protect your credit.

## If the Collectors Call

If you follow the advice contained in this book, you should never have to deal with collection calls on your student loans, because you will never become delinquent on your student loans. But, if you are already delinquent and are reading this book to find out how to resolve your situation, you need to know how to handle the calls as painlessly as possible. The first thing you need to do is swallow your anger. The caller is not harassing you. In fact, you gave them permission to call you when you signed your Master Promissory Note.

The second thing you need to do is swallow your pride. I know, from personal experience, how embarrassing it can be to have bill collectors calling you to ask when you will be paying your bill. If you had the money to pay it, you would have paid it already and they wouldn't be calling you. But the difference between default prevention specialists and regular bill collectors is; the bill collector's job is to collect the money, the default prevention specialist's job is to help you resolve your financial bind.

The call should follow a set pattern. The representative will ask you for payment. The best way to cure a delinquency is through payment. If you can scrape up the funds, this is in your best interests, as well as the lender's. After all, once you have paid the bill, you no longer owe it. If, as happens to so many of us from time to time, you have $25 to buy groceries for the remainder of the month, you probably won't be willing to send it to your student loan lender. Explain this to the representative. They eat too, and most of them have families to support and bills to pay. Remember, you are talking to a human being.

The second step in the call should be for the representative to begin asking you a series of rather personal questions. They aren't simply being nosy. They are trying to qualify you for a deferment – which is better for you financially than a forbearance. There may be enough notes in your file that the representative will know you do not qualify for deferment, but a good default prevention specialist will go over the possibilities anyway, just in case someone missed something on an earlier call.

The final solution offered should be forbearance, and the representative should find out from you when you expect to be able to resume making payments. Many lenders will only allow forbearance in increments of six months or one year, but if your lender has a more flexible policy, the representative will try to offer you every advantage possible. Take advantage of their expertise to explore all the options available to you. Pick their brains as thoroughly as possible to find a long-term solution.

One of my colleagues used to refer to forbearance as a band aid placed on arterial bleeding. It doesn't solve the problem, although it may help a little in the short run. So, while you are resolving the immediate problem – the current delinquency – try to determine how you will handle the ongoing problem. If you have lost your lender's telephone number or address, be sure to gather the information while you have the representative on the line. Remember, your student loans won't go away until you pay them, and ignoring the situation only makes it worse.

So, now you've heard my fifty cent lecture, and I sincerely hope you never get to talk to Pam or Mike or El, but if you do talk to them, let them help you. Good luck, folks.

# Additional Reading

## Research Your Options

For those of you just beginning the process, I recommend reading *Financial Aid 101* by Carlyn Foshee Chatfield. Ms. Foshee walks you through the process of applying for student financial aid – including the dreaded FAFSA. As the former Assistant Director for Student Financial Services at Rice University, she knows the 'ins and outs' of college funding better than you or I can ever hope to. Her book is designed to assist you in obtaining the funds needed to complete your education. She does not go into the difficulties of repaying those loans after you graduate. However, she includes an excellent chapter on state aid programs, and an even more exhaustive appendix with additional state programs. I would recommend it to anyone beginning their search for higher education funding, and certainly for anyone involved with high school students still considering their future.

Carlyn Foshee Chatfield, *Financial Aid 101*, Peterson's, 2004.
www.petersons.com

For those just beginning, and also for those who already have a heavy student loan debt burden, take a look at *1001 Ways to Pay for College* by Gen and Kelly Tanabe. Although this book does not go into the gory details on any of the programs mentioned, they do provide contact information. In something over 500 pages, you should be able to locate at least one program which will be helpful to you. In their chapter on loan forgiveness (immediately following their chapter on available loan programs), they list 61 different ways to get your student loans discharged, partially forgiven, or paid for you. It is definitely worth looking at (especially for teachers), and another of those books which should be on the shelf of every high school guidance counselor.

Gen and Kelly Tanabe, *1001 Ways to Pay for College*, SuperCollege, LLC, 2003. www.supercollege.com

There are actually a couple of other books currently on the market designed to help you manage your student loans. Although I was unable to find any of them in local bookstores, I did find them readily available on the internet at half.com. *Take Control of your Student Loan Debt,* by Robin Leonard and Deanne Loonin is one such book. Issued by Nolo, the 3rd edition is copyrighted 2001.

This book has a great deal of information concerning older student loans, and contact information for locating the current holder of your loans (if you are unable to locate them using the website provided in this book). Because much of the information is based on the older loans, you may not find sufficient data on post-1993 loans. You should definitely verify any information with your specific lender.

If you are already in default, this book has a wealth of information on how to protect yourself from the legal remedies available to your lender and the government. They also go into great detail regarding debt collection law.

If you attended a trade school, and believe you did not benefit from the training you received, Leonard and Loonin list some possible recovery techniques.

I will include a couple of caveats here. Leonard and Loonin recommend keeping a call log of any contact regarding your student loans. A call log is an excellent idea, since it will help you to keep track of things, and provide a memory jog regarding each contact. They also recommend you note the name of the person you spoke with, and *their direct telephone number*. Since most lenders and guarantors operate call centers, the person you spoke with is unlikely to have a direct line. And they are equally unlikely to be willing to provide you with their full name. Default prevention specialists – bill collectors – receive threats against their life and safety. Occasionally, those threats are put into action.

Leonard and Loonin also recommend you go on a fact finding mission before you identify yourself as a student loan borrower. *It is neither necessary nor advisable to lie to your lender or the guarantor about your identity when trying to gather information.* The default prevention specialist's job is to help you manage your loans. Frankly, they don't have time to waste on someone 'gathering information for an article in the college newspaper'. They are also not authorized to make statements of record for publication. So, if you try this tactic, the representative will as likely as not refer you to one of the many websites available with information regarding student loans and move on to a call where they can actually help someone.

Robin Leonard and Deanne Loonin, *Take Control of your Student Loan Debt,* Nolo, 2001, www.nolo.com.

Another of the books I located on half.com is *Free Yourself from Student Loan Debt – Get out from Under Once and for All* by Brian O'Connell. The copyright on this book is 2004, and the copy I purchased is clearly marked Uncorrected Proof – Not for Sale. Given that, we can assume much of what I read will be corrected before the book actually shows up in bookstores. The book was an easy read, and very useful in the area of personal finance and debt management. Unfortunately, O'Connell spends very little time dealing with the specifics of student loans. He goes into some depth on the importance of budgeting and the mechanics of setting up a budget. If you are unsure how to begin, he is an excellent resource. Beyond that, he states up to 100% of your student loan debt can be discharged because of public service. This is quite true – but only if all of your student loans are Perkins loans. Those discharges are not available on Stafford/Direct loans. There are numerous other *facts* presented which are either inaccurate or inadequately explained, so I would not recommend it as a resource for managing your *student loans*. However, as a personal debt management resource, it may be very valuable to you.

Brian O'Connell, *Free Yourself from Student Loan Debt – Get out from Under Once and for All*, Dearborn Trade Publishing, 2004,trade@dearborn.com.

Half.com is a wonderful source for locating out-of-print books. *The Guerrilla Guide to Mastering Student Loan Debt,* by Anne Stockwell, is the best of the student loan management books I found. Ms. Stockwell doesn't seem to have an agenda other than helping students and parents to manage their student loan burden. The book was published in 1997, and is therefore woefully out of date. The 1993 loan program changes are not incorporated into the book. However, if your loans pre-date 1993, the book is very useful. If you can find a copy, it is well-written and easy to read. Ms. Stockwell maintains an air of cheer throughout, despite the grim nature of her subject. Definitely worth the time and effort required to find a copy – for historical research if nothing else.

Anne Stockwell, *The Guerilla Guide to Mastering Student Loan Debt*, HarperCollins Publishers, Inc., 1997. www.harpercollins.com

**Useful Websites**

I have listed a few of the websites available to you. There are literally hundreds more. If you go on-line and begin to research your options, the pop-ups from lenders will drive you crazy, but it might be worth it if you find just the right lender to help you out. Begin with the federal sites and move on to the state sites and the lender sites.

Office of Student Financial Assistance, U. S. Department of Education – 800-433-3243
www.studentaid.ed.gov – federal website – Everything you need to know is available here.
www.dlssonline.com – Direct Loans – deferment and discharge forms for Stafford, Direct, and PLUS loans
www.studentclearinghouse.org – National Student Clearinghouse maintains enrollment records for in-school deferments.
www.fafsa.ed.gov – If you have not yet completed your FAFSA, get it online here.
www.nslds.ed.gov – National Student Loan Data System – central database for student aid.
www.ed.gov – Direct Loan information
www.salliemae.com – Tons of information including loan application forms and forbearance or deferment forms for those who have loans with SallieMae.
www.amsa.com – AMSA is a lender/guarantor. Again, tons of information on loans, including applications and repayment programs.
www.studentloan.citibank.com – Citibank website. Citibank does guaranteed student loans and private loans as well. Forms available here, including the latest MPN.
www.financialaid.com – Information on consolidation.

www.nelliemae.com – Complete information on student loans as well as applications online.

www.bhpr.hrsa.gov/nursing/loanrepay.htm – NERLP may cover up to 85% of your nursing loans.

www.mapping-your-future.org – I found clear explanations of loan forgiveness programs here, with links to forms.

www.upromise.com – New college savings program – join free – gives you a percentage of qualifying purchases as credit towards college costs.

www.finaid.org – This is a good site for finding out about your Expected Family Contribution.

www.collegiatefunding.com/calculator.html – This is another good site for calculating your EFC.

---

[xxxi] www.collegeloan.com
[xxxii] www.upromise.com
[xxxiii] www.usteas.gov/press/releases/js1512.htm

# Appendix A: Acronyms

AFDC – Aid to Families with Dependent Children

CNTP –Critical Needs Teacher Loan/Scholarship Program

DoE – Department of Education

EFC – Expected Family Contribution

EHD – Economic Hardship Deferment

FAFSA – Free Application for Federal Student Aid

FFELP/FFEL – Federal Family Education Loan Program

HEAL – Health and Education Assistance Loans

MPN – Master Promissory Note

NERLP – Nurse's Education Loan Repayment Program

NOAA – National Oceanic and Atmospheric Administration

PLUS loan – Parental Loan for Undergraduate Students

SLS – Federal Supplemental Loans for Students

SSI – Supplemental Security Income

UED – Unemployment Deferment

VISTA – Volunteers in Service to America

# Appendix B: Glossary

Acceleration – speeding up. When applied to loans it means the payment process speeds up and the loan can become *all* due and payable.

Accrue – to amass, grow or accumulate. When applied to your loans it means the interest is earned.

Amortize – to spread (payments) out over a period of time. A fully amortized loan has its payments set such that they will completely pay off the loan (principal and interest) in substantially equal payments over a specific period of time.

Capitalization – the process of turning interest into capital. When applied to your loans, the interest is added to the principal balance and thereafter becomes capital.

Compound interest – paying interest on interest. Interest is added to the principal balance as it accrues and is compounded on a regularly scheduled basis. In the case of an investment, this means the investor earns a somewhat higher rate of return than would be the case with simple interest. In the case of a *debt*, the borrower *pays* a somewhat higher rate of return than would be the case with simple interest.

Collection fees – fees earned in the forced collection of a debt. For student loans, these fees can range as high as 25% of the *original* principal balance.

Debit – to take away. When applied to your loans, may refer to taking a payment automatically from your checking or savings account (auto-debit) or may refer to applying a charge to your student account, as when a loan is first credited to your account and later removed for some reason.

Debt Service – the amount of money required to pay back a loan.

Default – a failure to fulfill an obligation. For student loans, default can occur when 270 days have passed without the lender receiving a scheduled monthly payment, or when 330 days have passed without payment if payments are scheduled less frequently than monthly.

Default Prevention Specialist – one who works diligently to prevent defaults, a bill collector. When used in reference to your student loan, the person trying to reach you by mail or telephone to inform you of your delinquency and offer you solutions to your financial difficulties.

Deferment – the process of delaying something. When applied to student loans, the federally authorized manners in which payment on your loans may be delayed.

Delinquency/delinquent – neglectful or failing in an obligation. On your student loans, being late in your scheduled payments.

Disbursement – that which is given out. In reference to your student loans, each disbursement constitutes a separate loan. You may have more than one disbursement each term.

Discharge – to unload, dismiss, or get rid of – As applied to student loans, when your debt is eliminated and you are relieved of the obligation to repay the loan because you have met certain conditions.

Dropping out – what Timothy Leary did in the sixties. The act of leaving school without the intention to return and finish a course of study.

Entitlement – something you have a right to and which cannot be denied to you. Deferments are an entitlement. If you meet the qualifications, the lender cannot refuse to defer your loans. Keep in mind, though, you must meet *all* of the qualifications, and all deferments carry time limitations.

Expected family contribution – what you borrowed because you had to. The amount of money the government expects a student's family to contribute to their higher education as determined by their Free Application for Federal Student Aid.

Enrollment – the act of formally entering into a program of study.

Federally insured – federal education loans not actually made by the government are insured by the government against default.  This is an inducement to the lenders which causes them to agree to make loans to students who have not yet shown themselves to be credit-worthy.  If the loans were not federally insured, the lenders would a) require a higher interest rate in order to make the loan, or b) decline to make the loan.

Forbearance – the act of refraining from pursuing a course of action; the lender's permission to take time off from making payments on student loans.  During periods of forbearance, the lender refrains from pursuing collection efforts despite non-payment of the loan.

Forgiveness – When applied to student loans, when the government pardons a borrower and relieves them of the obligation to repay their loan(s), generally because the borrower has performed public service.

Grant – to give.  In reference to student aid, funds made available to students for their education which do not have to be repaid under most circumstances.

Grace period – The most misunderstood concept in student loans.  The grace period is a period of time (6 months for Stafford/Direct/Ford loans, 9 months for Perkins loans) after the student drops below half-time enrollment, during which the loans are in a holding pattern.  The repayment cycle begins the day after the grace period lapses.  The grace period is a one time deal *for each disbursement*, and once used (in whole or in part) cannot be re-used.

Guarantor/guaranty agency – the private insuring agency from whom the federal government purchases the insurance for your student loans.  In the event of delinquency or default, the guarantor is required to perform collection efforts.

Original loan balance – The amount of money (plus the origination fee and guaranty fee) that you received to go to school. You likely received multiple disbursements.

Principal – money; the amount you borrowed, plus accrued and capitalized interest, less the amount (exclusive of interest) you have paid. That big chunk of money (debt) you are trying to pay off!

Promissory note – a promise to pay offered in exchange for a loan.

Right to sell or assign – the lender's right to transfer ownership of your debt to another lender, to the guaranty agency, or to the government. The lender is required to notify you if such a transfer takes place, but they are only obligated to send the notice via first class mail to the last address you gave them.

Simple interest – also called straight interest. A percentage of the principal debt which constitutes the price of borrowing money. Simple interest is applied periodically (usually annually), and you do not pay interest on interest already earned. Simple interest loans are generally available only from people who love you.

Skip tracing – the process of tracking down an individual who has 'skipped out' on their obligations.

Stopping out – a term used by financial aid professionals to describe the act of leaving school before completing your course of study. Stopping out may occur for a semester or for a period of years. When the student fails to enroll for the upcoming term, and yet fully intends to return at a later date and complete his or her course of study, the student is said to have 'stopped out'.

Subsidized – having a regular allowance or financial aid. In regard to student loans, the government pays the interest on subsidized loans during periods of deferment or other federally authorized delay of payment.

Total and permanent disability – Total and permanent disability is defined as the inability to work and earn money because of an illness or injury that is expected to continue indefinitely or to result in death. *The government will accept no lesser standard of disability when reviewing a case for discharge.*

Unsubsidized – without financial aid or subsidy. The government does not pay the interest on unsubsidized loans during periods of deferment or other authorized delay of payment.

Wage garnishment – the process by which some of your wages may be taken by the guarantor or the government (besides what they already take for taxes) before your employer cuts your paycheck each month. A situation to be avoided.

# Index